Instant Pot®

ELECTRIC PRESSURE COOKER COOKBOOK

Quick & Easy Recipes
for Everyday Eating

**SARA QUESSENBERRY &
KATE MERKER**

Instant Pot®

ELECTRIC PRESSURE COOKER COOKBOOK

Quick & Easy Recipes
for Everyday Eating

**SARA QUESSENBERRY &
KATE MERKER**

Race Point
PUBLISHING

Inspiring | Educating | Creating | Entertaining

Brimming with creative inspiration, how-to projects, and useful information to enrich your everyday life, Quarto Knows is a favorite destination for those pursuing their interests and passions. Visit our site and dig deeper with our books into your area of interest: Quarto Creates, Quarto Cooks, Quarto Homes, Quarto Lives, Quarto Drives, Quarto Explores, Quarto Gifts, or Quarto Kids.

© 2017 by Quarto Publishing Group USA Inc.

First published in 2017 by Race Point Publishing,
an imprint of The Quarto Group
142 West 36th Street, 4th Floor
New York, NY 10018 USA
T (212) 779-4972 F (212) 779-6058
www.QuartoKnows.com

Race Point titles are also available at discount for retail, wholesale, promotional, and bulk purchase. For details, contact the Special Sales Manager by email at specialsales@quarto.com or by mail at The Quarto Group, Attn: Special Sales Manager, 401 Second Avenue North, Suite 310, Minneapolis, MN 55401, USA.

ISBN 978-1-63106-333-6

Instant Pot® and the Instant Pot® logo are registered trademarks of Double Insight, Inc. and are used throughout this book with permission.

Photo on page 120 © Shutterstock/Brent Hofacker; photo on page 104 © Shutterstock/AS Food studio.

Text and Recipes: Sara Quessenberry and Kate Merker
Editorial Director: Jeannine Dillon
Project Editor: Erin Canning
Art Director: Merideth Harte
Photography: Evi Abeler
Food Stylist: Sara Quessenberry
Assistant Food Stylist: Monica Pierini
Design: 3&Co.

14 13 12 11

Printed in Canada

Contents

BEEF AND LAMB MAINS

POULTRY MAINS

PORK MAINS

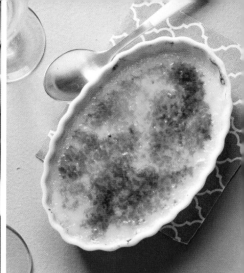

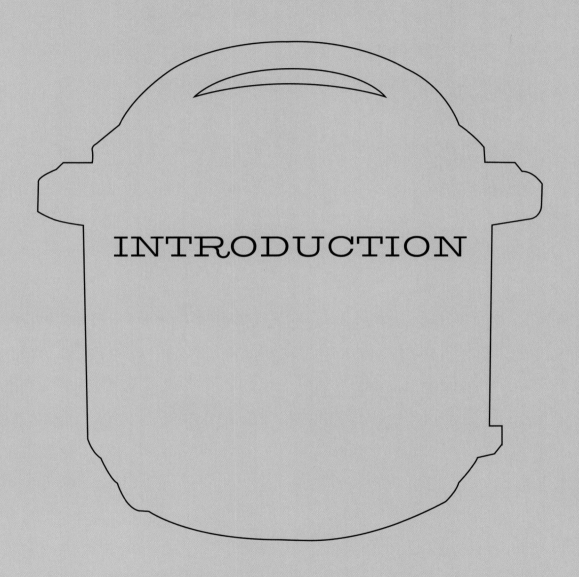

INTRODUCTION

So you finally got an Instant Pot® ...congratulations!

Perhaps you've read all the incredible reviews from bloggers, chefs, and home cooks and decided to get an Instant Pot®. Or maybe you have a friend who WON'T stop raving about it, and you caved and bought one of your own. Possibly, you received one as a gift.

Well, no matter how you got your Instant Pot®, you must now be wondering what you're supposed to do with this magical appliance. You've heard it can cook eggs, meat, pasta, rice, vegetables, cheesecake, and more, but you have no idea how to get started. Don't worry—you're not alone! We are here to help.

First off, we want to reassure you—the rumors are all true. With one pot, you can make Butterscotch-Pecan French Toast for breakfast (page 34), Crunchy Chicken Lettuce Cups for lunch (page 101), Deviled Eggs for an appetizer (page 40), Beef Ragù for dinner (84), and Chocolate–Peanut Butter Brownies for dessert (page 157). Oh, and it can make creamy, homemade yogurt, too.

In case you weren't sure, this is definitely not your grandmother's stovetop pressure cooker. It doesn't squeal. And it certainly won't explode. In fact, the Instant Pot® is an electric pressure cooker, and it is capable of so much more than those single-function pots from days of yore. Not only does it pressure-cook your food, often cutting cooking time at least by half (think dried beans in 45 minutes without soaking), it also has a built-in slow cooker for those days when you want dinner ready the moment you walk in the door after a long day.

So what's the difference between a pressure cooker and a slow cooker? With a pressure cooker, steam builds pressure, raising the boiling point, so food cooks faster. Translation: You can have stew on a school night and still have time to do homework.

"You can make stew on a school night and still have time to do homework!"

A slow cooker, on the other hand, uses low temperatures and a lot of time to cook a meal. In other words: Throw ingredients in and forget it. With the Instant Pot®, you get the best of both worlds. You don't just save time, you add diversity to meal planning and simplify your life in the kitchen by getting everything in a single appliance. No more cluttered countertops—HUGE bonus for anyone living in an apartment or home with a small kitchen!

The many functions of the Instant Pot® provide a versatility that you could never achieve with just a slow cooker or pressure cooker alone. Take the sauté mode (one of our favorites): Yes, it does the obvious, and sautés onions and garlic to bring out their true flavors (see Jambalaya on page 124); but it also sears meat to lock in flavor and form that desirable golden-brown crust (see Cranberry and Herb–Stuffed Turkey Breast on page 102); and it simmers sauces, so you can reduce them down to the perfect consistency (see Sticky and Sweet Sriracha Ribs on page 117). This book has all the recipes you need to get started using your Instant Pot®, including old-fashioned favorites, such as Pulled Pork Sandwiches (page 108) and Potato Salad with Mustard Vinaigrette (page 56). And it wil also give you the inspiration to stretch and experiment with delicious new flavors in dishes like Braised Lamb Souvlaki (page 81) and Pozole soup (page 118).

We also give you a breakdown on what you absolutely need to know about the Instant Pot®, including what the buttons do (page 16) and what rookie mistakes to avoid (page 17). We use everyday ingredients in the recipes, nothing exotic or difficult to find. But if you happen to come upon something you don't recognize, check out the list of pantry items (page 21) for a quick description.

Throughout the book, there are "button" icons at the top of each recipe. These indicate which function you will use on your Instant Pot® to cook the recipe. In the case of a few slow cook recipes, we also provide an alternative pressure cooked version of the recipe on the same page (just in case you don't want to wait 8 hours). Below are the button icons you'll see throughout the book, and you will find the corresponding buttons on your Instant Pot® for when you start cooking.

Hopefully, you will take comfort and pride in making these recipes and gain the know-how and inspiration to create new recipes of your own.

Before you know it, you'll want to cut back on take-out and fast foods, and get back to making quick and easy dinners every night at home. The Instant Pot® can handle the pressure so you don't have to!

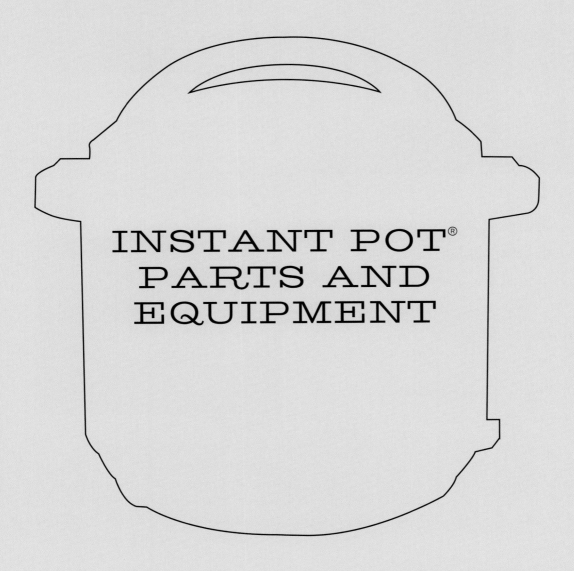

INSTANT POT® PARTS AND EQUIPMENT

To develop the delicious recipes in this book, we worked with the magnificent Instant Pot® DUO60 V2 (the 6-quart pot). Here is a quick breakdown of the parts and functions of the IP-DUO60 V2 as well as some tips and tricks when working with them.

POT HANDLES ▲

The pot handles also brilliantly double as a lid holder—the notches on either side of the lid fit perfectly into the slots of the pot handles. There's no need to take up sacred counter space when you can simply slide the lid into its holder.

FLOAT VALVE, EXHAUST VALVE, ANTI-BLOCK SHIELD ▲

These are located on the inside of the lid. When pressure is reached, the float valve (right) pops up and remains in the up position until the pressure is released; then it will drop and you will be able to open the lid. The exhaust valve (left) is protected by the metal anti-block shield (not pictured). The anti-block shield is designed to prevent food particles from interfering with the steam release valve. Always make sure that the float valve, exhaust valve, and anti-block shield are clean and free of food particles.

STEAM CONDENSATION COLLECTOR ▲

This small plastic container locks into place on the side of your Instant Pot® and collects any extra condensation that develops during cooking.

**PRESSURE RELEASE VALVE/
STEAM RELEASE HANDLE ▲**

This is the valve that seals in or releases steam. When pressure cooking, make sure that the valve is as close to "sealing" as possible. This is the only way that the pressure cooker can actually come up to pressure. This same valve is also what is used if your recipe calls for the "quick release" method for venting the steam. If it does call for this method, it simply means that you are to turn this handle toward "venting" when the recipe specifies. If you have been pressure cooking, doing this will make a considerable amount of noise and (very hot!) steam will come out of the three small slits on the top of the valve. When you use the slow cooker function, the valve should be in the "venting" position the entire time.

SILICONE SEALING RING ▲

This is the large, clear ring on the inside of the lid that prevents air from getting out of the pot when the lid is closed and locked. If it is not securely in place, it can change how long the Instant Pot® takes to reach pressure. Or you may not even be able to close the lid at all. Always keep the ring clean and free of food particles. (Tip: It absorbs odors and flavors and can impart whatever it has absorbed onto the next dish you make, so make sure to wash it between each use and consider buying an extra ring, and use one for savory dishes and the other for desserts.)

INNER POT AND STEAM RACK ▲

The inner pot is the stainless steel insert that sits inside the Instant Pot® and engages the heating element. It's where all the cooking happens. The steam rack is used to elevate food or your baking dish above the water in the bottom of the pot while pressure cooking.

What You Absolutely Need to Know Before Using Your Instant Pot®

We know some of you want to dive right in and get started using your Instant Pot®, so in this section, we have compiled the essential things you need to know to get started: how to release the steam when pressure cooking, the function of the buttons on the digital display, and the most common mistakes that rookies make—fortunately, we made them so you don't have to!

THE BUTTONS

> To change the time for any function, use the **+** or **−** keys to increase or decrease the desired time.

> The [**ADJUST**] button changes the slow cook temperature from "less" to "normal" to "more." It will also adjust the sauté temperature.

> Use the [**PRESSURE**] button to change the pressure setting between "low pressure" and "high pressure."

> When using the [**MANUAL**] setting, adjust to cook on low or high pressure by pressing the [Pressure] button. Then use **+** or **−** to set the time.

> To sauté, press the [**SAUTÉ**] button. It is automatically set to "Normal," which is what we used for all of our recipes. But if you would like less heat or more heat, press the [**ADJUST**] button to change between "Less", "Normal," or "More." When the temperature has been reached, the display will show "Hot." This is for open-lid cooking only.

> When slow cooking, press the [**SLOW COOK**] button and then the [**ADJUST**] button to select "Less," "Normal," or "More." Then use the **+** or **−** to adjust the time. For all of our slow cooker dinners, we used the "More" setting for 8 hours.

> To steam, press the [**STEAM**] button and then the [**PRESSURE**] button to adjust for low or high pressure. Then use the **+** or **−** to adjust the time.

> When using the Soup, Meat/Stew, Bean/Chili, or Poultry settings, each one has a specified pressure and amount of time. You can change them to high or low pressure by pressing the [**PRESSURE**] button, and you can change the time by using the **+** or **−** buttons.

QUICK RELEASE VS. NATURAL RELEASE

Once the timer has gone off and the pressure cooking has finished, you have two choices on how to release the steam:

"Quick Release" is when you open the steam release handle by turning it from "Sealing" to "Venting" to let the steam release very quickly (just be careful of the steam; it's extremely hot and there will be a lot of it).

"Natural Release" is when the timer goes off and you let the pressure release without doing anything. When the pressure cooking time has finished, the Instant Pot® automatically switches to the "Keep Warm" setting. During this time, the pressure begins to slowly drop. The amount of liquid and ingredients in the pot will determine how long this "Natural Release" process will take, but you can figure on at least 10 minutes and up to 20 minutes. Some recipes call for a "Natural Release" with a specific amount of time before venting the remaining steam.

ROOKIE MISTAKES

1. **Not setting the steam release valve to the locked position for pressure cooking and steaming.** If you don't lock it, pressure will never build.

2. **Not moving quickly enough.** When you open the steam release valve, do so in a very quick movement, or better yet, use a towel to release the valve because the steam escapes very quickly and it is extremely hot.

3. **Overfilling the pot.** It is best not to fill the pot more than two-thirds full (or one-half full for foods that expand, such as rice, pasta, and porridge), otherwise it could cause clogging, excess pressure, and leaking.

4. **Forgetting to add water for pressure cooking or steaming.** As a general rule, make it a habit to always fill your Instant Pot® with 1½ cups (350 ml) of water and insert the steam rack before you do anything else.

5. **Not attaching the condensation collector.** This could result in water slowly leaking over your countertop through the night as your food slowly cooks.

6. **Touching the lid while pressure cooking.** That thing is hot!

7. **Remembering to turn off your Instant Pot®.** Because the "Keep Warm/Cancel" button are the same, make sure to select the button when you finish preparing your meal. The display should switch to "Off."

ESSENTIAL
KITCHEN
TOOLS
AND
PANTRY
ITEMS

Now that you understand how your Instant Pot® works, it's time to get cooking! Here are the items that are great to have on hand when cooking with your Instant Pot®, as well as when making the recipes in this book.

KITCHEN TOOLS

These are the kitchen tools that we have found to be especially useful when cooking with the Instant Pot®.

ALUMINUM FOIL

Keep a roll handy because we ask you to use foil to cover the desserts before they go into the Instant Pot®. We also use foil to make a "sling" that helps lower a tight-fitting dish into the Instant Pot® and lift it out. To make a sling, tear off a 20-inch (51 cm) piece of foil and fold it over lengthwise into thirds (about 3 inches, or 7.5 cm, wide) to create a sturdy contraption that can be used multiple times.

METAL CAKE PANS

From the 6 x 3-inch (15 x 7.5 cm) round cake pan to the 7-inch (18 cm) tube and springform pans, these pans will suit your Instant Pot® baking needs.

MEASURING CUPS

The Instant Pot® itself contains lines of measurement, but we found it a little easier to use actual measuring cups when developing recipes and cooking.

SOUFFLÉ/CASSEROLE DISH

This versatile 8 x 3-inch (20 x 7.5 cm) round porcelain dish really maximizes the space in your Instant Pot®, fitting in just perfectly with little room to spare. Use it for desserts, such as the Lemon Soufflé Pudding Cake (page 159), or for savory main dishes, like the Layered Vegetable Casserole (page 136).

STEAMER BASKET

This inexpensive steamer is different from the steam rack that is included with your Instant Pot®. It has a collapsible basket that will expand to the size of your pot, maximizing the amount of vegetables you can steam. The holes are smaller, too, which means nothing will fall through (try using it for the Smashed Root Vegetables on page 67 or the Potato Salad with Mustard Vinaigrette on page 56).

TONGS

Tongs are one of the most efficient tools to have on hand. Use them to stir, turn, grab, pluck, and lift. We like the 9-inch (23 cm) size that locks closed for storage.

WOODEN SPOONS

Obviously, these are useful for all reasons spoon-related. But we particularly like a wooden spoon for scraping up the yummy brown bits from the bottom of the pot because it won't scratch it. Both rounded spoons and spoons that are squared off are recommended.

PANTRY ITEMS

These are the pantry items that are consistently used throughout this book. But these are also items that we use in our everyday cooking. You will find that most of these are basic things that you might already have in your kitchen.

BONE BROTH

More of a refrigerator or freezer staple, a bone broth is one of the most requested recipes for the Instant Pot®. Whether you prefer to use it for cooking or for sipping, the recipe on page 23 will cover all of your needs.

CANNED CHIPOTLES IN ADOBO

Chipotle peppers are smoked and dried red jalapeños that have been rehydrated and canned in a tangy-sweet red sauce (adobo). If you are looking for a smoky taste with just a bit of heat, scrape the seeds out of the chiles or consider just using the sauce without any chiles at all. Once you open the can, you can store the chiles and sauce in an airtight container for a few weeks.

CHILI GARLIC SAUCE

This is a bright red, fiery sauce with nearly the same ingredients as sriracha, but it boasts a delicious garlicky taste and has bits of chopped chiles in it.

COCONUT MILK

Don't confuse coconut milk with coconut water, which comes from the center of green coconuts. Coconut milk is made from grating and pressing the "meat" of brown coconuts. It has a mildly sweet flavor and creamy texture. Make sure to vigorously shake the can before opening it to combine the thick cream with the watery milk.

CRUSHED RED PEPPER FLAKES

This is a blend of a variety of chiles that have been dried and crushed, not ground. Look for a jar containing bright red flakes. If they are dull in color, that means the peppers have begun to lose their flavor.

DRY RED AND WHITE WINE

Cooking with wine won't get you drunk. Actually, the alcohol evaporates during the cooking process and leaves a greater depth of flavor, which can sometimes be sweet or acidic. As a rule of thumb, only cook with wines that you would drink. For white, we reach for Sauvignon Blanc or Pinot Grigio, and for red, we reach for Cabernet Sauvignon or Merlot.

EXTRA-VIRGIN OLIVE OIL

We use this oil for everything, from sautéing meats and vegetables to making vinaigrettes, to drizzling over dips, soups, and stews just before serving. We prefer "first cold press," which means that it was made simply by pressing the olives.

FRESH HERBS

If you ever feel like your dish is missing something, reach for a fresh herb like parsley, dill, rosemary, or thyme. Folding in chopped fresh herbs to nearly any dish will transform the ordinary to extraordinary.

FRESH LEMON

This may be one of the best-kept pantry-staple secrets. We always have lemons in our produce drawer and not just for flavoring our water. Squeezing a bit of juice over a dish just before serving adds a bright finish. We also use fresh lemon juice in vinaigrettes, pastas, and even on roasted vegetables. But before you juice that lemon, grate some of the zest to add an extra zip to dips, casseroles, and rice.

FRESHLY GROUND BLACK PEPPER

Don't waste your money on pre-ground pepper; the taste barely resembles pepper at all. For the real deal, grind your own peppercorns in a pepper mill as needed. Our favorite black peppercorns are Tellicherry.

KOSHER SALT

This is a coarse grain salt without any additives. We believe it has a purer taste than plain old table salt.

PARMESAN/PECORINO

When it comes to hard grating cheeses, Parmesan and Pecorino are the only two you need. What's the difference? Pecorino is a sheep's milk cheese. It has a saltier, sharper taste than Parmesan, which is made from cow's milk and is mild, yet rich, and has a slightly nutty taste and flaky texture. Pecorino comes from different regions in Italy, each with their own unique taste. But when reaching for Parmesan, the only choice for us is Parmigiano Reggiano.

PURE VANILLA EXTRACT

While pure vanilla extract comes with a higher price tag, the clean taste is worth every penny, especially in recipes where the flavor of vanilla will stand out.

RED THAI CURRY PASTE

This is an aromatic, concentrated paste made from lemongrass, red chiles, galangal (akin to ginger), and other spices. It is often mixed with coconut milk and is the base for many curries. You can find it in small jars in the Asian section of your grocery store.

SMOKED PAPRIKA

Smoked paprika is a specialty of Spain where the peppers are dried and slowly smoked over wood fires before being ground. This process creates an incredible red color and an intensely deep, rich, smoky flavor.

SRIRACHA

This is a tangy hot sauce made from chiles, vinegar, garlic, sugar, and salt. We use it as the base in the sauce for our ribs (see Sticky and Sweet Sriracha Ribs on page 117). But you can also use it to spice up your favorite condiments, whisk it into dipping sauces and vinaigrettes, or even use it on its own.

TAHINI

Made from ground sesame seeds, tahini is incredibly creamy, smooth, and delicious. Just like natural peanut butter, the oils in tahini separate, so make sure to stir it well before using. It is in our Hummus with Olives, Cucumber, and Tomatoes (see page 44), but consider mixing a spoonful into vinaigrettes or even smoothies.

Beef Bone Broth with Fresh Ginger

YIELD:
Makes 8 cups (1.9 L)
PREP TIME:
15 minutes
COOK TIME:
12 hours 15 minutes

INGREDIENTS

3 pounds (1.4 kg) beef bones, such as shin or femur, sawed into 2-inch (5 cm) pieces (ask your butcher)

9 cups (2.1 L) cold water

1 medium yellow onion, sliced into ½-inch-thick (13 mm) wedges

2 medium carrots, sliced into ½-inch-thick (13 mm) rounds

2 ribs celery, sliced into ½-inch-thick (13 mm) pieces

6 cloves garlic

8 sprigs fresh parsley

8 sprigs fresh thyme

2 tablespoons (32 g) tomato paste

2 teaspoons kosher salt

1 teaspoon black peppercorns

2 dried bay leaves

3-inch (7.5 cm) piece fresh ginger, divided

1. Put the bones and water into the Instant Pot®. Press [Sauté] and let the water come to a boil. Simmer the bones for 15 minutes and use a spoon to skim off and discard any foam that rises to the surface.

2. Add the onion, carrots, celery, garlic, parsley, thyme, tomato paste, salt, peppercorns, and bay leaves to the pot. Slice 2 inches (5 cm) of the ginger into ¼-inch-thick (6 mm) rounds and add to the pot. Press [Cancel]. Lock the lid. Press [Slow Cook], leave the vent open, and cook on "More" for 12 hours.

3. Place a fine mesh strainer in a large bowl. Discard the bones and vegetables, and strain the broth. Transfer the broth to a large storage container with a lid. Let the broth cool to room temperature then refrigerate it until cold.

4. To serve, first discard the solid layer of fat from the top of the broth, then heat the broth. Finely grate the remaining 1-inch (2.5 cm) piece ginger and stir into the broth. Serve hot.

BREAKFAST

Yogurt Parfaits with Apricot-Glazed Berries

YIELD:
4 servings
PREP TIME:
20 minutes
COOK TIME:
8 hours 5 minutes (plus 6 hours refrigeration time)

INGREDIENTS

YOGURT
3¾ cups (880 ml) whole milk
4 teaspoons whole-milk plain Greek yogurt (we used Fage Total; you may use any yogurt that has live and active cultures)

PARFAITS
2 tablespoons (40 g) apricot jam
1 tablespoon (15 ml) fresh lemon juice
8 ounces (225 g) fresh strawberries, hulled and cut into pieces
6 ounces (170 g) fresh blueberries
1 cup (113 g) granola

NOTE: You can make more yogurt by using three 16-ounce (475 ml) canning jars (that is the most that can fit on the steamer rack without worry of it tipping over). Just fill the jars up, leaving about ½ inch (13 mm) at the top, and plan on a bit more refrigeration time.

1. To make the yogurt, insert the steam rack into the Instant Pot®. Add 1½ cups (350 ml) water. Divide the milk among four 8-ounce (235 ml) canning jars and place on the rack. Place the jar lids (but not the rings) on top of each jar (covering them will ensure that no condensation or steam will drip into the jars).

2. Lock the lid and press [Steam] and cook for 1 minute. Use the "Natural Release" method for 5 minutes, then vent any remaining steam and open the lid.

3. Using oven mitts or canning tongs, carefully transfer the jars to a wire cooling rack and remove the lids (alternatively, leave the jars in the pot and carefully remove the lids). Let the milk cool, stirring occasionally, to 115°F (46°C). This will take at least 45 minutes (and likely double for 16-ounce, or 475 ml, jars; see Note left).

4. Once the milk in each jar has cooled to 115°F (46°C), spoon off and discard any skin that has formed on the top, then stir 1 teaspoon Greek yogurt into each jar. Place the jars back into the pot and cover with the lids (but not the rings). Lock the lid. Press [Yogurt] and cook for 8 hours. When it is finished, "Yogt" will appear on the display. Press [Cancel], then open the lid.

5. Remove the jars and use the rings to close the jars completely. Refrigerate until chilled, at least 6 hours or overnight.

6. To make the parfaits, in a medium bowl, whisk together the jam and lemon juice. Add the strawberries and blueberries and toss to coat.

7. In glasses or bowls, layer the yogurt with the granola and glazed berries.

YIELD:
2 servings
PREP TIME:
10 minutes
COOK TIME:
15 minutes

Shakshuka

INGREDIENTS

2 tablespoons (30 ml)
  extra-virgin olive oil
1 medium yellow onion, sliced
1 red bell pepper, sliced
1 clove garlic, finely chopped
½ teaspoon ground cumin
½ teaspoon paprika
1 can (14½ ounces, or 410 g)
  diced tomatoes
½ teaspoon kosher salt,
  plus more for serving
¼ teaspoon freshly ground
  black pepper, plus more
  for serving
⅛ teaspoon crushed red
  pepper flakes
4 large eggs
1 tablespoon (4 g) chopped
fresh flat-leaf parsley

1. Turn the Instant Pot® on to [Sauté]. Heat the olive oil and add the onion and bell pepper, and cook, stirring often, until beginning to soften, 3 to 4 minutes. Add the garlic, cumin, and paprika, and cook, stirring, for 1 minute more.

2. Add the tomatoes, salt, black pepper, and red pepper flakes. Press [Cancel]. Lock the lid. Press [Manual] and cook on high pressure for 8 minutes. Use the "Quick Release" method to vent the steam, then open the lid.

3. Use a spoon to make a well in the sauce, then crack an egg into it. Repeat with the remaining eggs. Lock the lid. Press [Manual] and cook on high pressure for 1 minute (for soft yolks). Use the "Quick Release" method to vent the steam, press [Cancel], then open the lid.

4. Divide the eggs and sauce among plates and season the eggs with a little more salt and black pepper. Sprinkle with the parsley and serve.

Asparagus and Parmesan Frittata

Manual

YIELD:
4 servings
PREP TIME:
15 minutes
COOK TIME:
25 minutes

INGREDIENTS

Olive oil, for the pan

8 large eggs

½ cup (115 g) sour cream

¾ teaspoon kosher salt

½ teaspoon freshly ground
black pepper

4 ounces (115 g) asparagus,
trimmed and cut into ¼-inch
(6 mm) pieces

2 scallions (white and light green
parts), thinly sliced

2 tablespoons (8 g) chopped
fresh flat-leaf parsley

¼ cup (25 g) plus 1 tablespoon
(5 g) grated Parmesan cheese,
divided

1. Insert the steam rack into the Instant Pot® and add 1½ cups
    (350 ml) water. Oil a deep 6- to 7-inch (15 to 18 cm) round
    cake pan or soufflé dish.

2. In a large bowl, beat the eggs, sour cream, salt, and pepper.
    Mix in the asparagus, scallions, parsley, and ¼ cup (25 g) of
    the Parmesan.

3. Transfer the mixture to the prepared pan and place on top of the
    steam rack. Lock the lid. Press [Manual] and cook on high pressure
    for 12 minutes. Use the "Natural Release" method for 10 minutes,
    then vent any remaining steam and open the lid.

4. Preheat broiler. Sprinkle the remaining 1 tablespoon (5 g)
    Parmesan over the top and broil until golden brown.

Quinoa Breakfast Bowl with Broiled Tomatoes

Multigrain

YIELD:
4 servings
PREP TIME:
15 minutes
COOK TIME:
15 minutes

INGREDIENTS

1 cup (173 g) quinoa

1½ cups (350 ml) water

¾ teaspoon kosher salt, divided

1 pint cherry tomatoes (25 to 30 tomatoes)

1 tablespoon (15 ml) extra-virgin olive oil

¼ teaspoon freshly ground black pepper

2 scallions (white and light green parts), thinly sliced

2 tablespoons (8 g) chopped fresh flat-leaf parsley

1 avocado

2 large eggs, hard-boiled, cooled, and peeled

1. Using a fine-mesh strainer, rinse the quinoa, then place in the Instant Pot®. Add the water and ½ teaspoon of the salt. Lock the lid. Press [Multigrain] and cook on high pressure for 7 minutes. Use the "Natural Release" method for 5 minutes, then vent any remaining steam and open the lid.

2. Fluff with a fork. Press [Cancel], lock the lid, and let sit for 5 minutes more.

3. While the quinoa is cooking, preheat broiler. On a small rimmed baking sheet, toss the tomatoes with the olive oil, pepper, and the remaining ¼ teaspoon salt. Broil until the tomatoes begin to burst, about 3 minutes. Toss with the scallions and parsley.

4. Pit, peel, and dice the avocado. Divide the quinoa among bowls, top with the tomatoes and avocado, then coarsely grate the eggs on top.

Overnight 5-Grain Cereal with Raspberries and Coconut

YIELD:

4 servings

PREP TIME:

5 minutes

COOK TIME:

8 hours

INGREDIENTS

½ cup (40 g) steel-cut oats

¼ cup (50 g) pearl barley

¼ cup (46 g) millet

2 tablespoons (13 g) wheat bran

2 tablespoons (14 g) flaxseed meal

3½ cups (825 ml) water

½ teaspoon pure vanilla extract

½ teaspoon kosher salt

Fresh raspberries, for serving

Toasted coconut, for serving

Honey, for serving

1. In the Instant Pot®, combine the oats, barley, millet, wheat bran, flaxseed meal, water, vanilla, and salt.

2. Lock the lid. Press [Slow Cook], leave the vent open, and cook on "More" for 8 hours.

3. Divide the cereal among bowls and top with raspberries, coconut, and honey.

Butterscotch-Pecan French Toast

YIELD:
4 servings
PREP TIME:
10 minutes
COOK TIME:
8 hours

INGREDIENTS

2 large eggs

1 cup (235 ml) half-and-half

1 teaspoon pure vanilla extract, divided

4 slices French or Italian bread, about 1 inch (2.5 cm) thick

3 tablespoons (45 g) unsalted butter

¾ cup (170 g) packed dark brown sugar

¼ cup (60 ml) heavy cream

½ cup (55 g) pecans, coarsely chopped

⅛ teaspoon kosher salt

1. In a large baking dish, whisk together the eggs, half-and-half, and ½ teaspoon of the vanilla. Add the bread slices and soak, flipping them halfway through, for about 5 minutes.

2. Turn the Instant Pot® on to [Sauté]. Add the butter and melt. Add the brown sugar and whisk until melted, about 30 seconds. Press [Cancel]. Whisk in the cream until incorporated and smooth, then whisk in the pecans, salt, and the remaining ½ teaspoon vanilla.

3. Add the bread slices to the pot, shaking off extra egg mixture before you do. Overlap to fit as necessary. Lock the lid. Press [Slow Cook], leave the vent open, and cook on "More" for 8 hours.

4. Serve the French toast butterscotch side up. Drizzle the extra sauce and pecans over the top.

Banana Bread

Manual

YIELD:
6 servings
PREP TIME:
10 minutes
COOK TIME:
50 minutes

INGREDIENTS

¼ cup (½ stick, or 60 g) unsalted butter, melted, plus more for the pan

1 cup (120 g) all-purpose flour

½ teaspoon baking powder

¼ teaspoon baking soda

½ teaspoon kosher salt

⅛ teaspoon ground cinnamon, plus more for dusting

2 large eggs

⅓ cup (65 g) sugar

⅓ cup (77 g) sour cream

½ teaspoon pure vanilla extract

2 large ripe bananas, 1 mashed and 1 sliced, divided

½ cup (55 g) pecans, chopped

1 large ripe banana, sliced

1. Insert the steam rack into the Instant Pot® and add 1½ cups (350 ml) water. Butter a 6 x 3-inch (15 x 7.5 cm) round cake pan.

2. In a medium bowl, whisk together the flour, baking powder, baking soda, salt, and cinnamon.

3. In a second medium bowl, whisk together the eggs, sugar, sour cream, melted butter, and vanilla. Mix in the mashed banana. Add the dry ingredients and mix to combine; stir in the pecans.

4. Scrape the batter into the prepared pan and cover with aluminum foil. Place the pan on the steam rack. Lock the lid.

5. Press [Manual] and cook on high pressure for 40 minutes. Use the "Quick Release" method to vent the steam, then open the lid.

6. Place the pan on a wire cooling rack and let cool for 10 minutes. Turn the bread out onto the rack and let cool completely. To serve, top with the sliced banana and dust with cinnamon.

APPETIZERS

YIELD:
12 pieces
PREP TIME:
20 minutes
COOK TIME:
6 minutes

Deviled Eggs

INGREDIENTS

6 large eggs

¼ cup (60 g) mayonnaise

1 tablespoon (15 ml) fresh lemon juice

1 teaspoon Dijon mustard

⅛ teaspoon freshly ground black pepper

Toppings: crumbled cooked bacon, chopped fresh herbs, sliced scallions or green beans, and ground spices such as cumin, curry powder, or smoked paprika

1. Insert the steam rack into the Instant Pot® and add 1½ cups (350 ml) water. Place 6 small canning jar rings or metal cookie cutters (any shape will work as long as the egg can sit inside) on the steam rack and place an egg in each one (this will keep them from rolling around).

2. Lock the lid. Press [Manual] and cook on low pressure for 6 minutes.

3. Use the "Quick Release" method to vent the steam, then open the lid. Immediately transfer the eggs to a bowl of ice water to cool.

4. In a medium bowl, whisk together the mayonnaise, lemon juice, mustard, and pepper.

5. Peel the eggs and slice them in half lengthwise. Scoop the yolks into the mayonnaise mixture and mash to combine. Spoon the mixture into the whites and sprinkle with desired toppings.

Smoky Glazed Chicken Wings

YIELD:
4 servings
PREP TIME:
15 minutes
COOK TIME:
15 minutes

INGREDIENTS

2 pounds (907 g) chicken wings, cut in half at the joint (about 24 pieces total)

1 teaspoon ground cumin

1 teaspoon ground coriander

1 teaspoon paprika

2 cans (6 ounces, or 175 ml, each) pineapple juice, divided

2 canned chipotle chiles in adobo sauce, finely chopped, plus 1 tablespoon (15 ml) adobo sauce

2 tablespoons (40 g) honey

1 tablespoon (11 g) Dijon mustard

1 lime, cut into wedges, for serving

1. In a large bowl, toss the chicken wings with the cumin, coriander, and paprika.

2. Insert the steam rack into the Instant Pot® and add all but ¼ cup (60 ml) of the pineapple juice. Evenly arrange the wings in the pot, standing them on end, if necessary.

3. Lock the lid. Press [Manual] and cook on high pressure for 8 minutes. Use the "Quick Release" method to vent the steam, then open the lid.

4. While the chicken is cooking, preheat broiler and line a large rimmed baking sheet with aluminum foil. In a large bowl, whisk together the chiles, adobo sauce, honey, mustard, and the reserved pineapple juice.

5. Transfer the wings to the bowl with the sauce and toss to coat. Arrange them in a single layer on the prepared baking sheet and broil until beginning to char, about 3 minutes per side. Serve with the lime wedges for squeezing over the wings.

Hummus with Olives, Cucumbers, and Tomatoes

YIELD:
4 servings

PREP TIME:
10 minutes

COOK TIME:
1 hour

INGREDIENTS

1 cup (250 g) dried chickpeas, rinsed

2 cloves garlic, peeled

¼ cup (60 g) sesame tahini

¼ cup (60 ml) fresh lemon juice

1¼ teaspoons kosher salt

1 teaspoon ground cumin

½ cup (120 ml) extra-virgin olive oil

¼ cup (60 ml) warm water

Kalamata olives, for serving

Diced cucumber, for serving

Diced tomato, for serving

Pita chips, for serving

1. In the Instant Pot®, combine the chickpeas and 4 cups (950 ml) water. Lock the lid. Press [Manual] and cook on high pressure for 45 minutes. Use the "Natural Release" method for 15 minutes, then vent any remaining steam and open the lid. Drain the chickpeas into a strainer and rinse under cold water to cool.

2. In a food processor, chop the garlic. Add the chickpeas, tahini, lemon juice, salt, and cumin. Process until a thick paste forms. With the motor running, slowly drizzle in the olive oil and let run until thick and creamy. Then drizzle in the water and purée until smooth and very creamy.

3. Spoon the hummus into a bowl and top with olives, cucumber, and tomatoes. Serve with pita chips.

Caramelized Onion Dip

YIELD:
1½ cups (375 g)
PREP TIME:
10 minutes
COOK TIME:
20 minutes

INGREDIENTS

2 tablespoons (30 g) unsalted butter

2 medium yellow onions, thinly sliced

¾ teaspoon kosher salt, divided

1 cup (230 g) sour cream

½ teaspoon Worcestershire sauce

3 fresh chives

Freshly ground black pepper, to taste

Potato chips, for serving

1. Turn the Instant Pot® on to [Sauté]. Melt the butter, then add the onions and ½ teaspoon of the salt, and stir to coat. Press [Cancel]. Lock the lid. Press [Manual] and cook on high pressure for 10 minutes. Use the "Quick Release" method to vent the steam, then open the lid.

2. Press [Sauté] and cook, stirring occasionally with a wooden spoon to scrape up the brown bits from the bottom of the pot, until the liquid has cooked away and the onions turn a golden brown, about 10 minutes. Transfer to a medium bowl and refrigerate until completely cool.

3. To the onions, add the sour cream, Worcestershire, and the remaining ¼ teaspoon salt, and stir well to combine. Using kitchen scissors, snip the chives into small pieces over the top and season with pepper. Serve with potato chips.

Chorizo and Pinto Bean Nachos

Sauté   Manual

YIELD:
4 servings
PREP TIME:
20 minutes
COOK TIME:
1 hour

INGREDIENTS

1 small red onion
1 tablespoon (15 ml) extra-virgin
    olive oil
8 ounces (225 g) fresh Mexican
    chorizo, casings removed
2 cloves garlic, finely chopped
½ teaspoon ground cumin
1 cup (250 g) dried pinto beans,
    rinsed
2½ cups (595 ml) water
3 tablespoons (45ml) fresh
    lime juice
¼ teaspoon kosher salt
¼ teaspoon freshly ground
    black pepper
6 ounces (170 g) tortilla chips
1½ cups shredded pepper
    Jack cheese (about 4 ounces,
    or 115 g)
6 radishes, thinly sliced
1 jalapeño, thinly sliced
½ cup (8 g) coarsely chopped
    fresh cilantro
Sour cream, for serving

1. Finely chop half the onion. Turn the Instant Pot® on to [Sauté]. Heat the olive oil. Add the chopped onion and chorizo, and cook, breaking up the chorizo into small pieces with a spoon and stirring occasionally until no longer pink, about 4 minutes.

2. Add the garlic and cumin and cook, stirring, for 1 minute. Add the beans and water. Press [Cancel]. Lock the lid. Press [Manual] and cook on high pressure for 35 minutes. Use the "Natural Release" method for 15 minutes, then vent any remaining steam and open the lid.

3. While the beans are cooking, thinly slice the remaining half onion and toss in a small bowl with the lime juice, salt, and pepper. Let sit, tossing occasionally, until ready to use.

4. Preheat broiler and line a large rimmed baking sheet with aluminum foil.

5. Arrange half the tortilla chips on the prepared baking sheet. Top with one-third of the cheese, then half the beans and another one-third of the cheese. Top with the remaining chips, beans, and cheese, and broil until the cheese melts, about 3 minutes.

6. Toss the onions with the radishes, jalapeño, and cilantro, then scatter over the nachos. Dollop with sour cream.

YIELD:
22 meatballs
PREP TIME:
20 minutes
COOK TIME:
10 minutes

Sweet-and-Sour Cocktail Meatballs

INGREDIENTS

MEATBALLS
1 pound (454 g) ground pork
   or chicken
4 scallions (white and light
   green parts), finely chopped,
   plus more for serving
2 tablespoons (16 g) finely
   grated fresh ginger
1 tablespoon (15 ml)
   less-sodium soy sauce
1 large egg white
½ teaspoon kosher salt

SAUCE
½ cup (120 ml) fresh
   orange juice
½ cup (120 ml) rice vinegar
¼ cup (50 g) sugar
5 to 6 teaspoons chili-garlic
   sauce
2 tablespoons (16 g) cornstarch
2 tablespoons (30 ml) water

1. To make the meatballs, in a large bowl, combine the pork, scallions, ginger, soy sauce, egg white, and salt. Mix with your hands until evenly incorporated. Using wet hands, shape the mixture into 22 small balls.

2. To make the sauce, in the Instant Pot®, whisk together the orange juice, vinegar, sugar, and chili-garlic paste. Press [Sauté] and bring the sauce to a boil. In a small bowl, whisk together the cornstarch and water. Once the sauce comes to a boil, slowly whisk in the cornstarch mixture. Press [Cancel]. Continue to whisk until the sauce stops boiling.

3. Add the meatballs to the sauce in a single layer. Lock the lid. Press [Manual] and cook on high pressure for 3 minutes. Use the "Quick Release" method to vent the steam, then open the lid.

4. Serve the meatballs and sauce sprinkled with scallions.

Blue Cheese Crostini with Bacon Jam

YIELD:
4 to 6 servings
PREP TIME:
20 minutes
COOK TIME:
30 minutes

INGREDIENTS

2 teaspoons extra-virgin olive oil

8 ounces (225 g) bacon, cut into ½-inch (13 mm) pieces

1 small onion, finely chopped

2 cloves garlic, finely chopped

¼ cup (60 ml) bourbon

2 tablespoons (30 ml) apple cider vinegar

2 tablespoons (30 ml) maple syrup

2 tablespoons (30 g) packed light brown sugar

¼ teaspoon crushed red pepper flakes

4 ounces (115 g) blue cheese

Crostini (½ large baguette, sliced and toasted), for serving

1. Turn the Instant Pot® on to [Sauté]. Add the olive oil and the bacon, and cook, stirring occasionally, for 6 minutes. Spoon off and discard all but 2 tablespoons (30 ml) of the drippings.

2. Add the onion and cook, stirring occasionally, for 3 minutes. Stir in the garlic and cook for 1 minute. Add the bourbon, vinegar, syrup, brown sugar, and red pepper flakes, and cook, scraping up any brown bits, for 1 minute. Press [Cancel].

3. Lock the lid. Press [Manual] and cook on high pressure for 10 minutes. Use the "Quick Release" method to vent the steam, then open the lid.

4. Press [Cancel], then press [Sauté] and simmer, stirring occasionally, until nearly all of the liquid has cooked away, 5 to 7 minutes. Spoon off and discard any excess fat. Spread the blue cheese on the crostini, then spoon the bacon jam on top.

Eggplant Caponata

YIELD:
4 cups
PREP TIME:
15 minutes
COOK TIME:
20 minutes

INGREDIENTS

¼ cup (35 g) pine nuts

¼ cup (60 ml) extra-virgin olive oil

1 medium red onion, chopped

2 ribs celery, thinly sliced

1 red bell pepper, cut into ½-inch (12 mm) dice

1 yellow bell pepper, cut into ½-inch (12 mm) dice

1 teaspoon kosher salt, divided

4 cloves garlic, finely chopped

1 large eggplant (about 1½ pounds, or 680 g), cut into ¾-inch (2 cm) dice

¼ cup (60 ml) red wine vinegar

3 tablespoons (48 g) tomato paste

5 teaspoons sugar

¼ teaspoon crushed red pepper flakes

¼ teaspoon freshly ground black pepper

¼ cup (25 g) chopped green olives

2 tablespoons (17 g) capers, drained

¼ cup (15 g) chopped fresh flat-leaf parsley

Crostini (½ large baguette, sliced and toasted), for serving

1. Turn the Instant Pot® on to [Sauté]. Add the pine nuts and toast, stirring often, until golden brown, 3 to 5 minutes. Transfer to a small bowl.

2. Heat the olive oil, then add the onion, celery, red bell pepper, yellow bell pepper, and ½ teaspoon of the salt, and cook, stirring often, until the vegetables begin to soften, 3 to 4 minutes. Stir in the garlic, then add the eggplant, and cook, stirring, for 1 minute.

3. In a small bowl, stir together the vinegar, tomato paste, sugar, red pepper flakes, black pepper, and the remaining ½ teaspoon salt. Stir into the vegetables until well coated. Press [Cancel].

4. Lock the lid. Press [Manual] and cook on high pressure for 10 minutes. Use the "Quick Release" method to vent the steam, then open the lid. Stir in the olives and capers and let cool to room temperature. Stir in the pine nuts and parsley. Serve with crostini.

Vegetable Pot Stickers with Sesame-Ginger Dipping Sauce

Sauté   Steam

YIELD:
30 pot stickers
PREP TIME:
45 minutes
COOK TIME:
20 minutes

INGREDIENTS

POT STICKERS

5 tablespoons (75 ml) canola oil, divided
8 ounces (225 g) shiitake mushrooms, caps sliced, stems discarded
1 tablespoon (15 ml) less-sodium soy sauce
3 scallions (white and light green parts), thinly sliced
1 small bunch of kale, thick stems and inner ribs discarded, leaves torn into pieces (about 6 cups, or 400 g)
½ teaspoon kosher salt
1 medium carrot, grated
30 square wonton wrappers
¾ cup (180 ml) water, divided

DIPPING SAUCE

½ cup (120 ml) less-sodium soy sauce
⅓ cup (80 ml) rice vinegar
2 tablespoons (30 ml) hot pepper sesame oil or toasted sesame oil
2 tablespoons (16 g) finely grated fresh ginger
2 teaspoons packed dark brown sugar

1. To make the filling, in a large skillet, heat 2 tablespoons (30 ml) of the canola oil over medium-high heat. Add the mushrooms and cook, stirring often, until tender, 3 to 4 minutes. Stir in the soy sauce and scallions. Add the kale and salt, and stir to coat. Reduce the heat to medium, cover tightly, and cook, stirring occasionally, until tender, 3 to 4 minutes. Stir in the carrot. Let cool.

2. To form the pot stickers, place a heaping teaspoon of the filling into the center of a wonton wrapper. Moisten the edges with water, fold over into a triangle, and press the edges tightly together to seal. Repeat with the remaining filling and wrappers.

3. To make the dipping sauce, in a small bowl, stir together the soy sauce, vinegar, sesame oil, ginger, and brown sugar.

4. Turn the Instant Pot® on to [Sauté]. Heat 1 tablespoon (15 ml) of the canola oil. Add a single layer of pot stickers (you should be able to fit 10) and cook until the undersides are golden brown, about 1 minute. Press [Cancel].

5. Add ¼ cup (60 ml) of the water. Lock the lid. Press [Steam] and cook for 3 minutes. Use the "Quick Release" method to release the steam, then open the lid. Transfer to a plate. Wipe out the pot and repeat steps 4 and 5 two more times with the remaining pot stickers, canola oil, and water.

6. Serve the pot stickers with the dipping sauce.

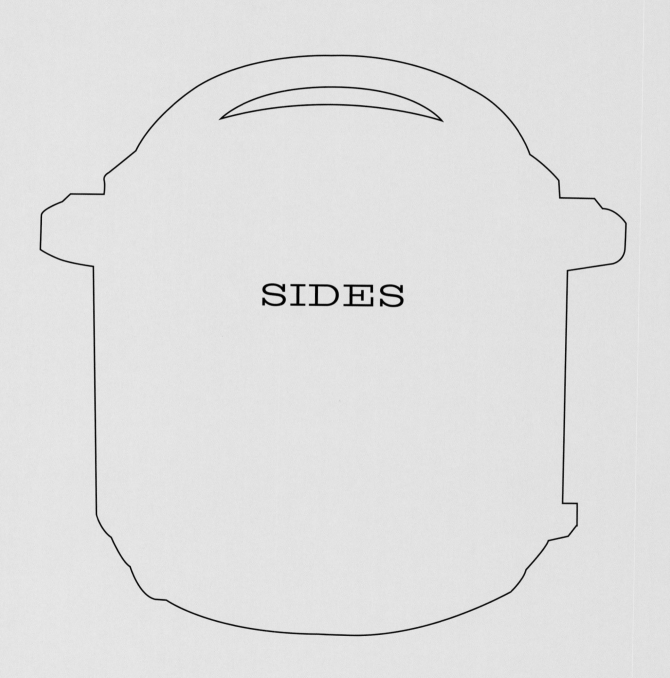

SIDES

Potato Salad with Mustard Vinaigrette

YIELD:
4 to 6 servings
PREP TIME:
15 minutes
COOK TIME:
8 minutes

INGREDIENTS

2 pounds (907 g) small new potatoes (about 16)

3 tablespoons (45 ml) extra-virgin olive oil

2 tablespoons (30 ml) red wine vinegar

1 tablespoon (11 g) whole-grain mustard

2 teaspoons Dijon mustard

2 half-sour pickles, cut into small pieces, plus 1 tablespoon (15 ml) brine

½ teaspoon kosher salt

¼ teaspoon freshly ground black pepper

½ medium red onion, thinly sliced

⅓ cup (20 g) coarsely chopped fresh flat-leaf parsley

1. Insert the steam rack or steamer basket into the Instant Pot® and add 1½ cups (350 ml) water. Place the potatoes on top of the basket and lock the lid. Press [Manual] and cook on high pressure for 8 minutes. Use the "Quick Release" method to vent the steam, then open the lid. Transfer the potatoes to a colander and run under cold water until cool enough to handle

2. In a large bowl, whisk together the oil, vinegar, mustard, brine, salt, and pepper, then stir in the onion.

3. Cut each potato into quarters, transfer to the bowl with the vinaigrette, and toss to coat. Add the pickles and parsley, and toss to combine.

Spaghetti Squash with Garlic and Sage Brown Butter

Sauté | Manual

YIELD:
4 servings
PREP TIME:
10 minutes
COOK TIME:
20 minutes

INGREDIENTS

1 spaghetti squash (about 3½ pounds, or 1.6 kg), halved crosswise and seeded

2 teaspoons packed light brown sugar

¼ teaspoon kosher salt

⅛ teaspoon freshly ground black pepper

⅛ teaspoon crushed red pepper flakes

¼ cup (½ stick, or 60 g) unsalted butter

2 cloves garlic, thinly sliced

12 fresh sage leaves

1. Insert the steam rack into the Instant Pot®. Add 1½ cups (350 ml) water.

2. Place the spaghetti squash halves on the steam rack. Lock the lid. Press [Manual] and cook on high pressure for 15 minutes. Use the "Quick Release" method to vent the steam, then open the lid. Press [Cancel].

3. In a small bowl, combine the brown sugar, salt, black pepper, and red pepper flakes. Set aside.

4. Lift out the squash. Using 2 forks, shred the squash into long strands and place on a large plate.

5. Pour out the water and dry the pot. Press [Sauté]. Melt the butter in the pot. Add the garlic and cook, stirring constantly, until light golden brown, about 1½ minutes. Add the sage and the brown sugar mixture and cook, stirring, until the sage is crisp, about 45 seconds.

6. Lift out the inner pot, spoon the sauce over the squash, and serve.

Twice-Baked Potatoes with Broccoli and Cheddar

Manual

YIELD:
4 servings
PREP TIME:
15 minutes
COOK TIME:
50 minutes

INGREDIENTS

4 russet potatoes (about 12 ounces, or 340 g, each)
1 bag (10 ounces, or 280 g) frozen broccoli, thawed and coarsely chopped
2 scallions (white and light green parts), finely chopped
1 cup (115 g) shredded Cheddar cheese, plus more for sprinkling
1 cup (230 g) sour cream
¾ teaspoon kosher salt
¼ teaspoon freshly ground black pepper

1. Insert the steam rack into the Instant Pot®. Add 1½ cups (350 ml) water.

2. Pierce the potatoes several times with a fork and place them on the steam rack. Lock the lid. Press [Manual] and cook on high pressure for 25 minutes. Use the "Natural Release" method for 15 minutes, then vent any remaining steam and open the lid.

3. Preheat oven to 450°F (230°C, or gas mark 8).

4. When cool enough to handle, make a slit in the top of each potato and carefully scoop out the potato flesh into a medium bowl, keeping the potato skin intact.

5. Mash the potatoes. Fold in the broccoli, scallions, Cheddar, sour cream, salt, and pepper. Spoon the mixture back into the potato skins and place on a rimmed baking sheet.

6. Sprinkle the tops with a little more cheese. Bake until the Cheddar melts and the filling is hot throughout, about 10 minutes.

Orange- and Honey-Glazed Carrots with Dill

YIELD:
4 servings
PREP TIME:
5 minutes
COOK TIME:
6 minutes

INGREDIENTS

¼ cup (60 ml) fresh orange juice

2 tablespoons (30 g) unsalted butter

¼ teaspoon kosher salt

8 medium carrots (about 1 pound, or 455 g)

1 tablespoon (20 g) honey

1 tablespoon (4 g) chopped fresh dill

1. To the Instant Pot®, add the orange juice, butter, and salt.

2. Slice the carrots at an angle into ½-inch-thick (13 mm) slices and add to the pot. Drizzle the carrots with the honey. Lock the lid. Press [Manual] and cook on high pressure for 3 minutes. Use the "Quick Release" method to vent the steam, then open the lid. Press [Cancel], then press [Sauté]. Simmer, stirring often, until the juice thickens and glazes the carrots, about 3 minutes.

3. Serve the carrots sprinkled with the dill.

Spice-Rubbed Cauliflower Steaks

Manual

YIELD:
4 servings
PREP TIME:
10 minutes
COOK TIME:
5 minutes

INGREDIENTS

1 large head cauliflower (about
    2 pounds, or 907 g)
2 tablespoons (30 ml) extra-virgin
    olive oil
2 teaspoons paprika
2 teaspoons ground cumin
¾ teaspoon kosher salt
¼ cup (4 g) chopped fresh
    cilantro
1 lemon, quartered

1. Insert the steam rack into the Instant Pot®. Add 1½ cups (350 ml) water.

2. Remove the leaves from the cauliflower and trim the core so the cauliflower sits flat. Place on the steam rack.

3. In a small bowl, combine the olive oil, paprika, cumin, and salt. Drizzle over the cauliflower and rub to coat.

4. Lock the lid. Press [Manual] and cook on high pressure for 4 minutes. Use the "Quick Release" method to vent the steam, then open the lid.

5. Lift the cauliflower onto a cutting board and slice into 1-inch-thick (2.5 cm) steaks. Divide among plates and sprinkle with the cilantro. Serve with the lemon quarters.

Marinated Beet Salad with Avocado, Grapefruit, and Blue Cheese

Manual

YIELD:
4 servings
PREP TIME:
15 minutes
COOK TIME:
25 minutes

INGREDIENTS

6 small to medium beets (red and golden), tops and bottoms trimmed

1 grapefruit

2 tablespoons (30 ml) extra-virgin olive oil

1 tablespoon (15 ml) white wine vinegar

2 teaspoons honey

¼ teaspoon kosher salt

⅛ teaspoon freshly ground black pepper

1 avocado

4 cups (220 g) baby salad greens

½ cup (60 g) crumbled blue cheese

8 fresh chives, snipped into small pieces with kitchen scissors

1. Insert the steam rack into the Instant Pot®. Add 1½ cups (350 ml) water.

2. Place the beets on the steam rack. Lock the lid. Press [Manual] and cook on high pressure for 25 minutes. Use the "Quick Release" method to vent the steam, then open the lid.

3. Over a bowl, section the grapefruit and squeeze out 3 tablespoons (45ml) of juice from the membranes. Set the grapefruit juice and sections aside.

4. To make the vinaigrette, whisk together the olive oil, vinegar, honey, salt, pepper, and reserved grapefruit juice.

5. When the beets are cool enough to handle, peel them (the skins should slip right off). Cut the beets into small wedges and place in a medium bowl. Toss them with ¼ cup (60 ml) of the vinaigrette and let marinate while they continue to cool to room temperature.

6. To assemble the salad, pit, peel, and quarter the avocado. Divide the baby greens, avocado, beets, reserved grapefruit sections, and blue cheese among bowls. Drizzle with the remaining vinaigrette and sprinkle with chives.

YIELD:
4 servings
PREP TIME:
15 minutes
COOK TIME:
35 minutes

Mexican Black Beans

INGREDIENTS

¼ bunch fresh cilantro

1 tablespoon (15 ml) extra-virgin olive oil

1 large onion, finely chopped

½ teaspoon kosher salt

½ teaspoon freshly ground black pepper

4 cloves garlic, finely chopped

1 teaspoon ground cumin

1 teaspoon dried oregano

1½ cups (375 g) dried black beans, rinsed

3 cups (700 ml) water

2 tablespoons (30 ml) sherry vinegar

Sliced scallions, for serving

Crumbled queso fresco, for serving

1. Finely chop the cilantro stems. Turn the Instant Pot® on to [Sauté]. Heat the olive oil and add the onion, salt, and pepper, and cook, stirring occasionally, for 5 minutes. Stir in the garlic, cumin, oregano, and cilantro stems, and cook for 1 minute.

2. Add the beans and water. Press [Cancel]. Lock the lid. Press [Manual] and cook on high pressure for 25 minutes.

3. Use the "Natural Release" method for 5 minutes, then vent any remaining steam and open the lid. Stir in the vinegar.

4. Transfer to a serving bowl and sprinkle with the scallions and cheese.

Smashed Root Vegetables

YIELD:
6 servings
PREP TIME:
15 minutes
COOK TIME:
20 minutes

INGREDIENTS

6 sprigs fresh thyme

2 sprigs fresh rosemary

6 cloves garlic, peeled

8 ounces (225 g) carrots, peeled and cut into 1-inch (2.5 cm) pieces

8 ounces (225 g) parsnips, peeled and cut into 1-inch (2.5 cm) pieces

12 ounces (340 g) rutabaga, peeled and cut into 1-inch (2.5 cm) pieces

1 pound (455 g) Yukon gold potatoes (about 4), peeled and quartered

¼ cup (60 ml) extra-virgin olive oil, plus more for drizzling

¾ teaspoon kosher salt

¼ teaspoon freshly ground black pepper, plus more for serving

1. Place the thyme and rosemary in the bottom of the Instant Pot®. Insert the steam rack into the pot and add 1½ cups (350 ml) water. Arrange the carrots on the rack, then top with the parsnips and rutabaga, followed by the potatoes.

2. Lock the lid. Press [Manual] and cook on high pressure for 10 minutes. Use the "Natural Release" method for 10 minutes, then vent any remaining steam and open the lid.

3. Transfer the vegetables to a bowl and coarsely mash together with the olive oil, salt, and pepper.

4. Drizzle with a little more olive oil, sprinkle with more pepper, and serve.

Creamy Rice with Poblanos and Corn

YIELD:
4 servings

PREP TIME:
15 minutes

COOK TIME:
20 minutes

INGREDIENTS

2 tablespoons (30 ml) extra-virgin olive oil

1 medium yellow onion, finely chopped

1 poblano chile, seeded and cut into ¼-inch (6 mm) pieces

½ teaspoon kosher salt

¼ teaspoon freshly ground black pepper

2 cloves garlic, finely chopped

1½ cups (293 g) long-grain white rice

1½ cups (350 ml) water

1 cup (163 g) fresh corn kernels

1 cup (230 g) sour cream

¼ cup (60 ml) fresh lime juice

½ cup (8 g) chopped fresh cilantro

1. Turn the Instant Pot® on to [Sauté]. Heat the olive oil. Add the onion, poblano, salt, and pepper, and cook, stirring occasionally, for 5 minutes. Add the garlic and cook, stirring, for 1 minute. Press [Cancel].

2. Stir in the rice and water. Lock the lid. Press [Manual] and cook on high pressure for 3 minutes. Use the "Natural Release" method for 10 minutes, then vent the remaining steam and open the lid.

3. Stir in the corn and cook for 1 minute. Press [Cancel]. Fold in the sour cream and lime juice, then fold in the cilantro. Serve immediately.

Garlicky Kale and Bacon

YIELD:
4 servings
PREP TIME:
15 minutes
COOK TIME:
10 minutes

INGREDIENTS

1 lemon

1 tablespoon (15 ml) extra-virgin olive oil

6 slices bacon, cut into 1-inch (2.5 cm) pieces

4 cloves garlic, thinly sliced

¾ cup (180 ml) less-sodium chicken broth

1 large bunch kale, thick stems and inner ribs discarded, leaves torn into pieces (about 12 cups, or 800 g)

½ teaspoon kosher salt, divided

½ teaspoon freshly ground black pepper, divided

1. Turn the Instant Pot® on to [Sauté]. Use a vegetable peeler to remove 2 strips of lemon zest. Thinly slice the zest and set aside.

2. Heat the olive oil. Add the bacon and cook, stirring occasionally, until the bacon is browned around the edges and crisp, 4 to 5 minutes. Transfer to a paper towel–lined plate and let cool.

3. Add the garlic and lemon zest to the pot and cook, stirring, for 1 minute. Add the chicken broth and half the kale, season with ¼ teaspoon each of the salt and pepper, and cook, tossing the kale until coated, about 1 minute. Add the remaining kale, season with the remaining ¼ teaspoon each salt and pepper, and toss to combine.

4. Press [Cancel]. Lock the lid. Press [Manual] and cook on high pressure for 4 minutes. Use the "Quick Release" method to vent the steam, then open the lid.

5. Toss the kale with the reserved bacon and transfer to a serving dish. Squeeze the juice of half the lemon on top just before serving.

Coconut Rice

YIELD:
4 servings
PREP TIME:
5 minutes
COOK TIME:
25 minutes

INGREDIENTS

1 tablespoon (8 g) sesame seeds

1½ cups (293 g) jasmine rice, rinsed

1 cup (235 ml) coconut milk

½ cup (120 ml) water

¼ teaspoon kosher salt

1 scallion (white and light green
parts), thinly sliced

1. Turn the Instant Pot® on to [Sauté]. Add the sesame seeds and toast, stirring often, until golden brown, 2 to 3 minutes. Press [Cancel]. Transfer to a small bowl.

2. In the Instant Pot®, combine the rice, coconut milk, water, and salt. Lock the lid. Press [Rice] and cook (the cooking time is automatically set). Use the "Natural Release" method for 10 minutes, then vent any remaining steam and open the lid.

3. Fluff the rice with a fork and serve sprinkled with the scallion and toasted sesame seeds.

YIELD:
4 servings
PREP TIME:
15 minutes
COOK TIME:
50 minutes

Three-Bean Salad

INGREDIENTS

¾ cup (188 g) dried kidney beans, rinsed

¾ cup (188 g) dried cannellini beans, rinsed

2 bay leaves

¼ cup (60 ml) fresh lemon juice

¼ cup (60 ml) extra-virgin olive oil

1 teaspoon chopped fresh rosemary

¾ teaspoon kosher salt

¼ teaspoon freshly ground black pepper

2 ribs celery, finely chopped

½ medium red onion, finely chopped

8 ounces (225 g) green beans, trimmed and cut into ¼-inch (6 mm) pieces

¼ cup (15 g) finely chopped fresh flat-leaf parsley

1. Place the kidney beans, cannellini beans, and bay leaves in the Instant Pot® along with 7 cups (1.6 L) water. Lock the lid. Press [Manual] and cook on high pressure for 30 minutes.

2. While the beans are cooking, in a large bowl, whisk together the lemon juice, olive oil, rosemary, salt, and pepper to make the vinaigrette. Add the celery and onion, and toss to combine.

3. Use the "Natural Release" method for 15 minutes, then vent any remaining steam and open the lid. Discard the bay leaves. Add the green beans and let stand for 5 minutes.

4. Drain the beans and run them under cold water to cool. Add them to the bowl with the celery and onion. Add the parsley and toss everything in the vinaigrette to combine.

Scallion Corn Bread

YIELD:
6 servings
PREP TIME:
10 minutes
COOK TIME:
40 minutes

INGREDIENTS

6 tablespoons (85 g) unsalted butter, melted, plus more for the pan and for serving

1 cup (125 g) all-purpose flour

½ cup (70 g) finely ground cornmeal

¼ cup (50 g) sugar

½ teaspoon baking powder

¼ teaspoon baking soda

½ teaspoon kosher salt

1 large egg

¾ cup (180 ml) buttermilk

1 scallion (white and light green parts), finely chopped

1. Insert the steam rack into the Instant Pot®. Add 1½ cups (350 ml) water.

2. Butter a 6 x 3-inch (15 x 7.5 cm) round cake pan. In a medium bowl, whisk together the flour, cornmeal, sugar, baking powder, baking soda, and salt.

3. In a large bowl, beat the egg, then whisk in the buttermilk and melted butter. Add the flour mixture to the egg mixture and mix until fully incorporated, then fold in the scallion.

4. Scrape the batter into the prepared pan and cover with aluminum foil. Place the pan on the steam rack.

5. Lock the lid. Press [Manual] and cook on high pressure for 35 minutes. Use the "Quick Release" method to vent the steam, then open the lid. Transfer the pan to a wire cooling rack and let cool for 5 minutes. Serve warm with butter.

BEEF
AND
LAMB
MAINS

Apple Cider and Thyme-Braised Brisket

YIELD:
6 servings
PREP TIME:
15 minutes
COOK TIME:
1 hour 10 minutes

INGREDIENTS

1 tablespoon (15 ml) extra-virgin olive oil

2½ pounds (1.1 kg) beef brisket

1½ teaspoons kosher salt

½ teaspoon freshly ground black pepper

6 cloves garlic, smashed

2 tablespoons (32 g) tomato paste

1 cup (235 ml) apple cider

2 tablespoons (30 ml) apple cider vinegar

1 tablespoon (20 g) honey

8 sprigs fresh thyme

3 tablespoons (12 g) chopped fresh flat-leaf parsley

3 tablespoons (12 g) chopped fresh dill

1. Turn the Instant Pot® on to [Sauté]. Heat the olive oil. Season the brisket with the salt and pepper. Add to the pot and cook until browned, about 5 minutes per side. Transfer to a plate.

2. Add the garlic to the pot and cook, stirring, for 30 seconds. Add the tomato paste, apple cider, vinegar, honey, and thyme, and cook for 1 minute, stirring and scraping up any brown bits from the bottom of the pot. Press [Cancel].

3. Add the brisket to the pot. Lock the lid. Press [Manual] and cook on high pressure for 55 minutes. Use the "Quick Release" method to vent the steam, then open the lid.

4. Transfer the brisket to a cutting board and let rest for a few minutes. Press [Cancel], then press [Sauté]. Discard the thyme sprigs. Let the sauce thicken to the desired consistency.

5. Thinly slice the brisket against the grain and transfer to a platter. Spoon the sauce over the top and sprinkle with the parsley and dill.

YIELD:
4 servings
PREP TIME:
15 minutes
COOK TIME:
45 minutes

Braised Lamb Souvlaki

INGREDIENTS

1 lemon

1 tablespoon (2 g) finely chopped fresh rosemary

2 teaspoons paprika

2 teaspoons ground cumin

½ teaspoon ground coriander

¾ teaspoon kosher salt, divided

¾ teaspoon freshly ground black pepper, divided

1½ pounds (680 g) boneless leg of lamb, trimmed and cut into 3-inch (7.5 cm) pieces

2 tablespoons (30 ml) extra-virgin olive oil, divided

2 cloves garlic, finely chopped

1 cup (235 ml) less-sodium chicken broth

2 tablespoons (32 g) tomato paste

¼ small red onion, thinly sliced

2 plum tomatoes, cut into wedges

¼ cup (25 g) pitted Kalamata olives, halved

4 flatbreads, warmed

Plain yogurt, for serving (see page 26 for instructions on how to make yogurt)

¼ cup (37 g) crumbled feta cheese

1. Using a vegetable peeler, remove 3 strips of zest from the lemon and thinly slice crosswise. Set aside.

2. In a small bowl, combine the rosemary, paprika, cumin, coriander, ½ teaspoon of the salt, and ½ teaspoon of the pepper. Rub the mixture all over the lamb [to coat].

3. Turn the Instant Pot® on to [Sauté]. Heat 1 tablespoon (15 ml) of the olive oil. Add the lamb and cook until browned on all sides, about 5 minutes total. Add the garlic and cook, stirring, for 1 minute. Add the chicken broth, tomato paste, and lemon zest, and cook, stirring, for 1 minute. Press [Cancel]. Lock the lid.

4. Press [Manual] and cook on high pressure for 40 minutes. Use the "Quick Release" method to vent the steam, then open the lid. Using 2 forks, shred the lamb and toss it in the cooking liquid.

5. Twenty minutes before the lamb is finished, place the onion in a medium bowl. Squeeze the juice of half the lemon on top and toss to combine. Let sit for 5 minutes. Add the tomatoes, olives, and the remaining 1 tablespoon (15 ml) olive oil, ¼ teaspoon salt, and ¼ teaspoon pepper, and toss to combine.

6. Spread each flatbread with some yogurt, then top with the lamb and the tomato salad. Sprinkle the crumbled feta cheese on top before serving.

YIELD:

6 servings

PREP TIME:

15 minutes

COOK TIME:

15 minutes

Chili Dogs

INGREDIENTS

1 tablespoon (15 ml) extra-virgin
    olive oil

1 medium red onion, finely
    chopped, divided

8 ounces (225 g) lean ground
    beef

1 tablespoon (7.5 g) chili powder

2 teaspoons ground cumin

1/8 teaspoon ground cinnamon

1 can (14½ ounces, or 410 g)
    crushed tomatoes

2 tablespoons (22 g) yellow
    mustard

1 tablespoon (15 g) light brown
    sugar

1 teaspoon Worcestershire sauce

6 hot dogs

1 half-sour pickle, chopped, plus
    2 tablespoons (30 ml) brine

2 tablespoons (8 g) chopped
    fresh flat-leaf parsley

Shredded Cheddar cheese,
    for serving

6 hot dog buns

1. Turn the Instant Pot® on to [Sauté]. Heat the olive oil, add all but 2 tablespoons (20 g) of the onion, and cook, stirring occasionally, for 5 minutes. Add the beef and cook, breaking it up into small pieces until no longer pink, about 4 minutes. Stir in the chili powder, cumin, and cinnamon, and cook for 1 minute.

2. Add the tomatoes, mustard, brown sugar, and Worcestershire, and stir to combine. Press [Cancel]. Nestle the hot dogs in the chili. Lock the lid. Press [Manual] and cook on high pressure for 2 minutes. Use the "Quick Release" method to vent the steam, then open the lid.

3. Meanwhile, in a small bowl, combine the pickle, brine, parsley, and the reserved onion.

4. Nestle the hot dogs in buns and top with the chili and Cheddar. Serve with the pickle-onion relish.

YIELD:
4 to 6 servings
PREP TIME:
20 minutes
COOK TIME:
50 minutes

Moroccan Lamb and Couscous Stew

INGREDIENTS

1 tablespoon (15 ml) extra-virgin olive oil

2 pounds (907 g) lamb shoulder, cut into 1½-inch (4 cm) pieces

1 teaspoon kosher salt

½ teaspoon freshly ground black pepper

1 medium yellow onion, thinly sliced

3 cloves garlic, finely chopped

2 teaspoons paprika

1½ teaspoons ground cumin

½ teaspoon ground cinnamon

6 medium carrots, cut into 3-inch (7.5 cm) sticks

1 tablespoon (8 g) finely grated fresh ginger

½ cup (120 ml) water

1 lemon

¾ cup (131 g) couscous

8 dried apricots, coarsely chopped

¼ cup (37 g) roasted almonds, coarsely chopped

¼ cup (4 g) chopped fresh cilantro

1. Turn the Instant Pot® on to [Sauté]. Heat the olive oil. Season the lamb with the salt and pepper. In batches, cook the lamb until browned on all sides, about 5 minutes. Transfer to a plate.

2. Add the onion to the pot and cook, stirring, for 2 minutes. Add the garlic, paprika, cumin, and cinnamon, and cook, stirring, for 1 minute. Add the carrots, ginger, and water. Using a vegetable peeler, peel 3 strips of lemon zest from the lemon and add to the pot. Add the lamb. Press [Cancel].

3. Lock the lid. Press [Manual] and cook on high pressure for 25 minutes. Use the "Quick Release" method to vent the steam, then open the lid. Press [Cancel]. Stir in the couscous and apricots. Lock the lid and let stand for 10 minutes.

4. Divide the stew among bowls and serve topped with the almonds and cilantro.

YIELD:
4 servings
PREP TIME:
25 minutes
COOK TIME:
8 hours 15 minutes (slow cook)
55 minutes (pressure cook)

Beef Ragù

INGREDIENTS

2 tablespoons (30 ml) extra-virgin olive oil, divided, plus more if necessary

1½ pounds (680 g) chuck steak, trimmed and cut into 2-inch (5 cm) pieces

¾ teaspoon kosher salt

½ teaspoon freshly ground black pepper

1 large yellow onion, chopped

4 cloves garlic, finely chopped

2 tablespoons (32 g) tomato paste

2 medium carrots, cut into ¼-inch (6 mm) pieces

1 rib celery, cut into ¼-inch (6 mm) pieces

1 cup (235 ml) dry red wine, such as Cabernet Sauvignon

1 can (28 ounces, or 795 g) whole peeled tomatoes, drained and crushed with your hands

2 anchovy fillets, chopped

2 sprigs fresh rosemary

2 sprigs fresh sage

12 ounces (340 g) pappardelle or other wide pasta

Grated Parmesan cheese, for serving

1. Turn the Instant Pot® on to [Sauté]. Heat 1 tablespoon (15 ml) of the olive oil. Season the beef with the salt and pepper. Add half the beef to the pot and cook until browned, about 5 minutes total. Transfer to a plate. Repeat with the remaining beef, adding more olive oil to the pot, if necessary.

2. Add the remaining 1 tablespoon (15 ml) olive oil and the onion, and cook, stirring occasionally, for 3 minutes. Add the garlic and cook, stirring, for 1 minute. Stir in the tomato paste and cook for 1 minute.

3. Add the carrots, celery, and wine, and cook, scraping up any brown bits, for 1 minute. Add the tomatoes followed by the anchovies, rosemary, and sage. Return the meat to the pot. Press [Cancel]. Lock the lid.

4. In this step, you have the option to slow-cook or pressure-cook (don't do both!). **To slow-cook:** Press [Slow Cook], leave the vent open, and cook on "More" for 8 hours. **To pressure-cook:** Press [Manual] and cook on high pressure for 40 minutes. Use the "Quick Release" method to vent the steam, then open the lid.

5. Twenty minutes before serving, cook the pasta according to the package directions.

6. Open the lid and discard the rosemary and sage. Press [Cancel], then press [Sauté] and simmer until the sauce is slightly thickened, about 5 minutes.

7. Using 2 forks, break the meat into slightly smaller pieces. Toss the ragù with the pasta and serve sprinkled with Parmesan.

Chili-Garlic Beef with Quick-Pickled Cucumbers

YIELD:
4 servings
PREP TIME:
20 minutes
COOK TIME:
45 minutes

INGREDIENTS

2 tablespoons (30 ml) canola oil

2 pounds (907 g) chuck steak, trimmed and cut into 1½-inch (4 cm) pieces

1½ teaspoons five-spice powder

½ cup (120 ml) less-sodium soy sauce

¾ cup (180 ml) water

¼ cup (60 g) plus 1 tablespoon (15 g) packed light brown sugar, divided

1 tablespoon (8 g) plus 1 teaspoon finely grated fresh ginger, divided

2½ teaspoons chili-garlic sauce, divided

2 large cloves garlic, finely chopped

¼ cup (60 ml) rice vinegar

1 seedless cucumber, thinly sliced

¼ small sweet onion, thinly sliced

1 tablespoon (8 g) cornstarch

1 tablespoon (15 ml) water

White rice, for serving

1 tablespoon (8 g) toasted sesame seeds, for serving

1. Turn the Instant Pot® on to [Sauté]. Heat the canola oil. Season the beef with the five-spice powder. Working in batches, cook the beef until browned on all sides, about 5 minutes. Transfer to a plate.

2. Meanwhile, in a small bowl, combine the soy sauce, water, ¼ cup (60 g) of the brown sugar, 1 tablespoon (8 g) of the ginger, and 2 teaspoons of the chili-garlic sauce. Stir until the sugar dissolves.

3. Add the garlic to the pot and cook, stirring, for 1 minute. Add the soy sauce mixture and cook, scraping up any bits on the bottom of the pot. Press [Cancel]. Return the beef to the pot and lock the lid. Press [Manual] and cook on high pressure for 30 minutes. Use the "Quick Release" method to vent the steam, then open the lid.

4. While the beef is cooking, make the cucumbers. In a medium bowl, whisk together the vinegar with the remaining 1 tablespoon (15 g) brown sugar, 1 teaspoon ginger, and ½ teaspoon chili-garlic sauce. Add the cucumber and onion, and toss to combine.

5. In a small bowl, combine the cornstarch with the water. Add to the pot, then turn the pot on to [Sauté] and simmer until slightly thickened, about 3 minutes. Serve the beef and sauce over the rice and top with the pickled cucumbers and sesame seeds.

YIELD:
4 servings
PREP TIME:
20 minutes
COOK TIME:
8 hours 15 minutes (slow cook)
1 hour (pressure cook)

Ropa Vieja

INGREDIENTS

1½ pounds (680 g) flank steak

1¼ teaspoons kosher salt, divided

½ teaspoon freshly ground black pepper

1 tablespoon (15 ml) extra-virgin olive oil

1 medium yellow onion, thinly sliced

1 red bell pepper, thinly sliced

1 green bell pepper, thinly sliced

4 cloves garlic, finely chopped

1½ teaspoons ground cumin

1 tablespoon (16 g) tomato paste

1 can (14½ ounces, or 410 g) diced tomatoes

½ teaspoon dried oregano

1 bay leaf

½ cup (50 g) pitted green olives

White rice, for serving

¼ cup (4 g) chopped fresh cilantro

1. Cut the flank steak in half crosswise so each piece can lie flat in the bottom of the pot. Season the halves with ¾ teaspoon of the salt and the pepper.

2. Turn the Instant Pot® on to [Sauté]. Heat the olive oil. Add one of the steak halves and sear until browned, 2 to 3 minutes per side. Transfer to a plate. Repeat with the remaining half.

3. Add the onion and red and green bell peppers to the pot, and cook, stirring and scraping up the brown bits from the bottom of the pot, until the vegetables begin to soften, 3 to 4 minutes. Add the garlic, cumin, and tomato paste, and cook, stirring, for 1 minute. Add the tomatoes, oregano, bay leaf, olives, and the remaining ½ teaspoon salt. Nestle the steak in the sauce. Press [Cancel]. Lock the lid.

4. In this step, you have the option to slow-cook or pressure-cook (don't do both!). To slow-cook: Press [Slow Cook], leave the vent open, and cook on "More" for 8 hours. To pressure-cook: Press [Manual] and cook on high pressure for 45 minutes. Use the "Quick Release" method to vent the steam, then open the lid.

5. Discard the bay leaf. Using two forks, shred the meat in the sauce. Serve the Ropa Vieja with rice and sprinkle with the cilantro.

YIELD:
4 servings
PREP TIME:
15 minutes
COOK TIME:
20 minutes

Mediterranean Stuffed Tomatoes

INGREDIENTS

1 lemon

2 tablespoons (30 ml) extra-virgin olive oil

1 small yellow onion, finely chopped

2 cloves garlic, finely chopped

1 tablespoon (2 g) fresh thyme leaves

12 ounces (340 g) lean ground beef

¾ teaspoon kosher salt, divided

½ teaspoon freshly ground black pepper, divided

½ cup (120 ml) dry white wine, such as Pinot Grigio

2 tablespoons (8 g) chopped fresh flat-leaf parsley

2 ounces (55 g) feta cheese, crumbled

4 large beefsteak tomatoes

Mixed green salad, for serving

1. Finely grate the zest of the lemon. Turn the Instant Pot® on to [Sauté]. Heat the olive oil. Add the onion and cook, stirring often, until tender and beginning to turn golden brown, 8 to 10 minutes. Stir in the garlic and thyme, and cook for 1 minute.

2. Add the beef, ½ teaspoon of the salt, and ¼ teaspoon of the pepper, and cook, breaking up the meat with a spoon, until browned, 6 to 8 minutes. Add the wine and simmer for 2 minutes. Press [Cancel]. Transfer the beef to a bowl and squeeze the juice of the lemon over the top. Add the lemon zest, parsley, and feta, and gently toss to combine.

3. Wipe out the pot, then insert the steam rack and add ½ cup (120 ml) water.

4. Using a sharp knife and working on an angle, remove the tomato stem from each tomato, leaving a 2-inch-wide (5 cm) opening in the tomatoes. With a spoon, scoop out most of the seeds and pulp (without breaking the skin). Season the inside of the tomatoes with the remaining ¼ teaspoon salt and ¼ teaspoon pepper. Divide the meat mixture among the tomatoes (about a heaping ½ cup, or 113 g, each).

5. Place the tomatoes on the rack. Lock the lid. Press [Manual] and cook on high pressure for 1 minute. Use the "Quick Release" method to vent the steam, then open the lid. Serve the stuffed tomatoes with a mixed green salad.

Balsamic Beef Short Ribs

YIELD:
4 servings

PREP TIME:
20 minutes

COOK TIME:
1 hour

INGREDIENTS

1 tablespoon (15 ml) extra-virgin olive oil

8 bone-in beef short ribs (about 3½ pounds, or 1.6 kg)

1½ teaspoons kosher salt

½ teaspoon freshly ground black pepper

6 cloves garlic, smashed

1 can (14½ ounces, or 410 g) crushed tomatoes

½ cup (120 ml) balsamic vinegar

½ cup (120 ml) water

8 sprigs fresh thyme

2 bay leaves

1 medium yellow onion, quartered

1¼ pounds (570 g) whole baby potatoes (about 16)

3 tablespoons (12 g) chopped fresh flat-leaf parsley

1 teaspoon finely grated lemon zest

1. Turn the Instant Pot® on to [Sauté]. Heat the olive oil. Season the short ribs with the salt and pepper. Add half of the ribs to the pot and cook until browned, about 3 minutes per side. Transfer to a plate. Repeat with the remaining short ribs.

2. Add the garlic to the pot and cook, stirring, for 30 seconds. Add the tomatoes, vinegar, water, thyme, and bay leaves.

3. Nestle the short ribs and onion into the sauce and place the potatoes on top. Press [Cancel]. Lock the lid. Press [Manual] and cook on high pressure for 45 minutes. Use the "Quick Release" method to vent the steam, then open the lid.

4. Divide the potatoes among plates and smash them with the back of a fork. Place the short ribs and onions on top of the potatoes. Discard the bay leaves and thyme sprigs. Spoon some of the sauce over the short ribs and sprinkle with the parsley and lemon zest.

POULTRY
MAINS

YIELD:
6 servings
PREP TIME:
30 minutes
COOK TIME:
45 minutes

Enchiladas Rancheras

INGREDIENTS

1 tablespoon (15 ml) plus ⅓ cup (80 ml) canola oil, divided

½ medium white onion, chopped

2 cloves garlic, smashed

2 pounds (907 g) beefsteak tomatoes, quartered and cored

1 serrano chile, seeded

2 ancho chiles, seeded

1¼ teaspoons kosher salt

¼ cup (60 ml) water

4 bone-in chicken breasts (about 3 pounds, or 1.4 kg)

12 corn tortillas

Crumbled queso fresco, for serving

Sliced avocado, for serving

Sliced red onion, for serving

Fresh sprigs cilantro, for serving

1   Turn the Instant Pot® on to [Sauté]. Heat 1 tablespoon (15 ml) of the canola oil. Add the onion and garlic, and cook, stirring often, for 2 minutes. Add the tomatoes, serrano chile, ancho chiles, salt, and water, and stir to combine. Place the chicken breasts on top of the tomato mixture. Press [Cancel].

2. Lock the lid. Press [Manual] and cook on high pressure for 15 minutes. Use the "Quick Release" method to vent the steam, then open the lid. Transfer the chicken to a bowl and, when cool enough to handle, shred the meat, discarding the skin and bones.

3. Meanwhile, fry the tortillas: Heat the remaining ⅓ cup (80 ml) canola oil in a small skillet over medium heat. Working with 1 tortilla at a time, cook for 15 seconds per side, then transfer to a paper towel–lined plate.

4. Using a handheld immersion blender (or a regular blender), purée the tomato mixture. Press [Sauté] and simmer the sauce until it thickens to the desired consistency (or until it reduces to about 3½ cups, or 825 ml). Spoon ½ cup (120 ml) of the sauce into the chicken in the bowl and toss to combine.

5. Preheat oven to 375°F (190°C, or gas mark 5).

6. Spread a thin layer of sauce over the bottom of a 13 x 9-inch (33 x 23 cm) baking dish. Dividing evenly, roll the chicken up in the tortillas and place seam side down in the baking dish. Smother with the remaining sauce. Bake until the sauce bubbles, 10 to 15 minutes.

7. Serve the enchiladas topped with cheese, avocado, onion, and cilantro.

Lemon Chicken with Green Olives

YIELD:
4 servings
PREP TIME:
15 minutes
COOK TIME:
25 minutes

INGREDIENTS

1 tablespoon (15 ml) extra-virgin olive oil

8 bone-in, skin-on chicken thighs (about 3 pounds, or 1.4 kg)

¾ teaspoon kosher salt

½ teaspoon freshly ground black pepper

4 cloves garlic, thinly sliced

1 medium yellow onion, thinly sliced

1 lemon, sliced into thin rounds

1 cup (100 g) pitted green olives

6 sprigs fresh thyme

2 tablespoons (8 g) chopped fresh flat-leaf parsley

1. Turn the Instant Pot® on to [Sauté]. Heat the olive oil. Pat the chicken dry with paper towels and season with the salt and pepper. Add half of the chicken, skin side down, and cook until the skin is golden brown and crisp, about 10 minutes. Flip the chicken and cook for 1 minute more. Transfer to a plate and repeat with the remaining chicken.

2. Add the garlic to the pot and cook, stirring, for 30 seconds. Add the onion, lemon, olives, and thyme, and cook, scraping up the brown bits from the bottom of the pot, for 2 minutes. Lay the chicken on top. Press [Cancel].

3. Lock the lid. Press [Manual] and cook on high pressure for 10 minutes. Use the "Quick Release" method to vent the steam, then open the lid.

4. Serve the chicken with the onions, lemons, and olives, and sprinkle with the parsley.

YIELD:
4 servings
PREP TIME:
25 minutes
COOK TIME:
25 minutes

Hunter-Style Chicken

INGREDIENTS

3 tablespoons (45 ml) extra-virgin olive oil, divided, plus more if necessary

10 ounces (280 g) cremini mushrooms, trimmed and quartered

4 bone-in chicken breasts, halved crosswise (about 3 pounds, or 1.4 kg)

¾ teaspoon kosher salt

½ teaspoon freshly ground black pepper

1 medium yellow onion, chopped

4 cloves garlic, finely chopped

1 large carrot, peeled and sliced ¼ inch (6 mm) thick

½ cup (120 ml) dry red wine, such as Cabernet Sauvignon

8 sprigs fresh thyme

1 can (28 ounces, or 795 g) whole peeled tomatoes, drained

Chopped fresh flat-leaf parsley, for serving

Crusty bread, for serving

1. Turn the Instant Pot® on to [Sauté]. Heat 1 tablespoon (15 ml) of the olive oil. Add the mushrooms and cook, stirring occasionally, until beginning to brown, about 4 minutes. Transfer to a plate.

2. Heat 1 tablespoon (15 ml) of the olive oil. Pat the chicken dry with paper towels and season with the salt and pepper. Add half the chicken, skin side down, and cook until the skin is golden brown and crisp, 4 to 6 minutes. Flip and cook for 1 minute more. Transfer to a plate. Repeat with the remaining chicken, adding more olive oil to the pot, if necessary.

3. Add the remaining 1 tablespoon (15 ml) olive oil and the onion, and cook, stirring occasionally, for 3 minutes. Add the garlic and cook, stirring, for 1 minute.

4. Add the carrot and wine, and cook, stirring and scraping up any brown bits on the bottom of the pot, for 1 minute. Add the thyme and tomatoes, crushing them with your hands as you add them to the pot. Add the mushrooms and mix to combine. Press [Cancel].

5. Arrange the chicken on top of the tomato mixture. Lock the lid. Press [Manual] and cook on high pressure for 10 minutes. Use the "Quick Release" method to vent the steam, then open the lid.

6. Serve the chicken and vegetables sprinkled with parsley and crusty bread alongside.

YIELD:
4 servings
PREP TIME:
15 minutes
COOK TIME:
25 minutes

Chicken Marbella

INGREDIENTS

8 bone-in, skin-on chicken thighs
(about 3 pounds, or 1.4 kg)
1 teaspoon dried oregano
¾ teaspoon kosher salt
½ teaspoon freshly ground black
pepper
1 tablespoon (15 ml) extra-virgin
olive oil, plus more if necessary
3 tablespoons (45 ml) red wine
vinegar
2 tablespoons (30 g) packed
light brown sugar
1 tablespoon (9 g) capers, plus
1 tablespoon (15 ml) brine
4 cloves garlic, thinly sliced
½ cup (120 ml) dry white wine,
such as Pinot Grigio
¾ cup (131 g) pitted prunes,
halved
½ cup (50 g) pitted green olives
Chopped fresh flat-leaf parsley,
for serving

1. Turn the Instant Pot® on to [Sauté]. Pat the chicken dry with paper
    towels and season with the oregano, salt, and pepper.

2. Heat the olive oil. Add half of the chicken, skin side down, and
    cook until the skin is golden brown and crisp, 8 to 10 minutes.
    Flip and cook for 1 minute more. Transfer to a plate and repeat
    with the remaining chicken (adding more olive oil to the pot if
    necessary).

3. Meanwhile, in a small bowl, whisk together the vinegar,
    brown sugar, and caper brine.

4. Add the garlic to the pot and cook, stirring, for 30 seconds.
    Add the wine and cook, stirring and scraping up any brown bits,
    for 1 minute. Add the vinegar mixture along with the prunes,
    olives, and capers. Press [Cancel].

5. Nestle the chicken in the olive mixture. Lock the lid. Press
    [Manual] and cook on high pressure for 10 minutes. Use the
    "Quick Release" method to vent the steam, then open the lid.

6. Serve the chicken with the olives, prunes, and a bit of the juices,
    and sprinkle with parsley.

Crunchy Chicken Lettuce Cups

Manual

YIELD:
4 servings
PREP TIME:
20 minutes
COOK TIME:
10 minutes

INGREDIENTS

1 piece (2 inches, or 5 cm) fresh
   ginger
2 cloves garlic, smashed
1 small red chile, seeded,
   if desired, and thinly sliced
3 tablespoons (45 ml)
   less-sodium soy sauce, divided
4 boneless, skinless chicken
   breasts (6 ounces, or 170 g,
   each)
¼ cup (60 ml) fresh lime juice
2 tablespoons (30 g) packed dark
   brown sugar
1 large crisp red apple (such as
   Braeburn, Honeycrisp, or Gala),
   cored and cut into thin ½-inch
   (13 mm) pieces
2 scallions (white and light green
   parts), thinly sliced
2 tablespoons (12 g) thinly sliced
   fresh mint
1 small head Boston lettuce,
   leaves separated
Chopped roasted peanuts,
   for serving

1. Finely grate enough ginger to get 1 teaspoon, then thinly slice the rest. Set aside the grated ginger.

2. Add the sliced ginger, garlic, half of the chile, 2 tablespoons (30 ml) of the soy sauce, and ½ cup (120 ml) water to the Instant Pot®. Insert the steamer rack.

3. Place the chicken on the rack. Lock the lid. Press [Manual] and cook on high pressure for 6 minutes. Use the "Natural Release" method for 5 minutes, then vent any remaining steam and open the lid. Transfer the chicken to a plate and let rest for 5 minutes. When cool enough to handle, shred into small pieces.

4. In a medium bowl, whisk together the lime juice, brown sugar, grated ginger, and the remaining 1 tablespoon (15 ml) soy sauce. Stir in the remaining chile.

5. Add the chicken and toss to coat. Add the apple, scallions, and mint, and toss to combine. Spoon the chicken mixture into the lettuce leaves and top with peanuts.

Cranberry and Herb-Stuffed Turkey Breast

YIELD:
4 to 6 servings
PREP TIME:
25 minutes
COOK TIME:
40 minutes

INGREDIENTS

¼ cup (30 g) dried bread crumbs

¼ cup (15 g) chopped fresh flat-leaf parsley

2 tablespoons (5 g) chopped fresh sage

2 teaspoons chopped fresh rosemary

2 cloves garlic, finely chopped

½ cup (60 g) dried cranberries, finely chopped

1½ teaspoons kosher salt, divided

¾ teaspoon freshly ground black pepper, divided

¼ cup (60 ml) extra-virgin olive oil, divided

1 boneless turkey breast (3 pounds, or 1.4 kg)

1 teaspoon paprika

¼ cup (60 ml) dry white wine, such as Pinot Grigio

1. In a small bowl, combine the bread crumbs, parsley, sage, rosemary, garlic, cranberries, ¼ teaspoon of the salt, ⅛ teaspoon of the pepper, and 3 tablespoons (45 ml) of the olive oil. Stir well to combine.

2. Butterfly the turkey breast: Place the breast on a cutting board, skin side down. Using a chef's knife, hold the blade parallel to the board and slice into the breast, starting at the thickest part. Cut along the length of the breast but not all the way through. Open it up like a book.

3. Season the inside with ¼ teaspoon of the salt and ⅛ teaspoon of the pepper. Spoon the stuffing onto the center of the breast, spreading evenly from top to bottom. Starting with one long side, roll the breast into a log so the stuffing is tightly enclosed. Use 5 lengths of butcher's twine to tie up the breast at 2-inch (5 cm) intervals along the length of the breast. Season the outside with the paprika and the remaining 1 teaspoon salt and ½ teaspoon pepper.

4. Turn the Instant Pot® on to [Sauté]. Heat the remaining 1 tablespoon (15 ml) olive oil. Add the turkey and cook until all sides are golden brown, 10 to 12 minutes. Add the wine. Press [Cancel].

5. Lock the lid. Press [Manual] and cook on high pressure for 30 minutes. Use the "Quick Release" method to vent the steam, then open the lid. Transfer the turkey to a cutting board and let rest for 5 minutes before slicing.

Colombian Chicken Soup

Manual

YIELD:
4 servings
PREP TIME:
10 minutes
COOK TIME:
20 minutes

INGREDIENTS

1 medium yellow onion,
  cut in half

2 medium carrots, cut in half
  crosswise

2 ribs celery, cut in half crosswise

3 bone-in chicken breasts (about
  2 pounds, or 907 g)

5 cups (1.2 L) water

1½ teaspoons kosher salt

1½ pounds (680 g) Yukon gold
  potatoes, cut into ½-inch
  (13 mm) pieces

1 ear corn, cut into 4 pieces

¼ teaspoon freshly ground black
  pepper

1 avocado

¼ cup (60 g) sour cream

1 tablespoon (9 g) capers, rinsed

1 teaspoon dried oregano

8 sprigs fresh cilantro

1 lime, quartered

1. To the Instant Pot®, add the onion, carrots, celery, chicken, water, and salt. Lock the lid. Press [Manual] and cook on high pressure for 15 minutes. Use the "Quick Release" method to vent the steam, then open the lid. Transfer the chicken to a large bowl. When cool enough to handle, shred into pieces, discarding the skin and bones.

2. Discard the onion, carrots, and celery. Add the potatoes and corn to the broth. Lock the lid. Press [Manual] and cook on high pressure for 2 minutes. Use the "Quick Release" method to vent the steam, then open the lid. Stir in the chicken and pepper.

3. Divide the soup among bowls. Peel, pit, and slice the avocado. Top the soup with the avocado, sour cream, capers, oregano, and cilantro. Serve with the lime quarters for squeezing.

PORK MAINS

Pulled Pork Sandwiches

YIELD:
4 servings
PREP TIME:
20 minutes
COOK TIME:
8 hours 20 minutes (slow cook)
1 hour 5 minutes (pressure cook)

INGREDIENTS

SPICE RUB
1 tablespoon (15 g) packed dark brown sugar
2 teaspoons chili powder
2 teaspoons ground cumin
1 teaspoon kosher salt
¼ teaspoon ground cinnamon
¼ teaspoon cayenne pepper
2 pounds (907 g) pork shoulder or butt, trimmed and cut into 3-inch (7.5 cm) pieces

SAUCE
1 cup (240 g) ketchup
¼ cup (85 g) unsulfured molasses
½ cup (120 ml) water
¼ cup (60 ml) apple cider vinegar
2 tablespoons (30 g) packed dark brown sugar
1 tablespoon (7.5 g) chili powder
1 tablespoon (11 g) Dijon mustard
2 teaspoons Worcestershire sauce
⅛ teaspoon cayenne pepper
1 tablespoon (15 ml) extra-virgin olive oil
1 medium yellow onion, thinly sliced
2 cloves garlic, finely chopped

SANDWICHES
4 rolls or buns, split
Your favorite coleslaw

1. To make the spice rub, in a small bowl, combine the brown sugar, chili powder, cumin, salt, cinnamon, and cayenne. Season the pork with the rub.

2. To make the sauce, in a medium bowl, whisk together the ketchup, molasses, water, vinegar, brown sugar, chili powder, mustard, Worcestershire, and cayenne.

3. Turn the Instant pot on to [Sauté]. Heat the olive oil. Add the onion and cook, stirring occasionally, for 3 minutes. Stir in the garlic and cook for 1 minute. Add the sauce and mix to combine. Press [Cancel].

4. Add the pork to the sauce and turn to coat. Lock the lid. Here you have the option to slow-cook or pressure-cook (don't do both!). To slow-cook: Press [Slow Cook], leave the vent open, and cook on "More" for 8 hours. To pressure-cook: Press [Manual] and cook on high pressure for 45 minutes. Use the "Quick Release" method to vent the steam, then open the lid.

5. Transfer the pork to a bowl. Press [Cancel], then press [Sauté] and simmer the sauce, stirring occasionally, until thickened, 3 to 5 minutes. Press [Cancel].

6. Using 2 forks, shred the pork, then return it to the pot and toss to coat. Pile the pork and coleslaw on the bottom halves of the buns and sandwich with the tops.

Hoppin' John Stew

Sauté | Manual

YIELD:
4 servings
PREP TIME:
20 minutes
COOK TIME:
30 minutes

INGREDIENTS

2 tablespoons (30 ml) extra-virgin olive oil, divided

14 ounces (395 g) kielbasa, sliced into ½-inch-thick (13 mm) pieces

1 large yellow onion, chopped

4 cloves garlic, finely chopped

1½ cups (325 g) dried black-eyed peas, rinsed

3 cups (700 ml) less-sodium chicken broth

1 jalapeño, sliced

4 scallions (white and light green parts), thinly sliced

4 cups (120 g) baby spinach

White rice, for serving

Hot sauce, for serving

1. Turn the Instant Pot® on to [Sauté]. Heat 1 tablespoon (15 ml) of the olive oil. Add half the kielbasa and cook, turning once, until browned, 3 to 4 minutes. Transfer to a plate. Repeat with the remaining 1 tablespoon (15 ml) olive oil and kielbasa.

2. Add the onion and cook, stirring occasionally, for 3 minutes. Stir in the garlic and cook for 1 minute.

3. Add the black-eyed peas, broth, jalapeño, and kielbasa. Press [Cancel].

4. Lock the lid. Press [Manual] and cook on high pressure for 12 minutes. Use the "Natural Release" method for 10 minutes, then vent any remaining steam and open the lid.

5. Fold in the scallions and spinach. Serve over rice with hot sauce.

Italian Sausage Meatballs

YIELD:
4 servings
PREP TIME:
20 minutes
COOK TIME:
25 minutes

INGREDIENTS

1 tablespoon (15 ml) extra-virgin olive oil

1 medium onion, finely chopped

1 large egg

2 tablespoons (30 ml) water

½ teaspoon kosher salt, divided

½ teaspoon freshly ground black pepper, divided

½ cup (60 g) panko bread crumbs

½ cup (50 g) grated Parmesan cheese, plus more for serving

¼ cup (15 g) chopped fresh flat-leaf parsley

3 cloves garlic, finely chopped

12 ounces (340 g) lean ground beef

8 ounces (225 g) sweet Italian sausage, casings removed

1 teaspoon dried oregano

2 tablespoons (32 g) tomato paste

1 can (28 ounces, or 795 g) crushed tomatoes

4 sprigs fresh basil, plus leaves for serving

4 slices country bread, toasted, for serving

Ricotta cheese, for serving

Mixed green salad, for serving

1. Turn the Instant Pot® on to [Sauté]. Heat the olive oil. Add the onion and cook, stirring occasionally, until beginning to soften, 5 to 6 minutes.

2. While the onions are cooking, in a large bowl, beat the egg with the water, ¼ teaspoon of the salt, and ¼ teaspoon of the pepper; stir in the bread crumbs. Add the Parmesan, parsley, and one-third of the garlic, and mix to combine. Add the beef and sausage, and mix until everything is fully incorporated. Shape the mixture into 25 balls (about 1½ inches, or 4 cm, in diameter each).

3. Stir the oregano and the remaining two-thirds garlic, ¼ teaspoon salt, and ¼ teaspoon pepper into the onions, and cook for 1 minute. Add the tomato paste and cook, stirring, for 1 minute. Add the tomatoes and basil sprigs to the pot, and stir to combine. Press [Cancel].

4. Place the meatballs on top of the sauce. Lock the lid. Press [Manual] and cook on high pressure for 7 minutes. Use the "Natural Release" method for 10 minutes, then vent any remaining steam and open the lid.

5. Meanwhile, spread the toasted bread with ricotta and divide among plates.

6. Spoon the meatballs and sauce over the bread and sprinkle with additional Parmesan and fresh basil leaves. Serve with a green salad.

Beer Garden Casserole

YIELD:
6 servings
PREP TIME:
10 minutes
COOK TIME:
40 minutes

INGREDIENTS

1 small Savoy or green cabbage (about 1½ pounds, or 680 g), cored

1 Granny Smith apple, cored and thinly sliced

2 pounds (907 g) sweet Italian sausage, casings removed

Dijon mustard, for serving

Chopped fresh dill, for serving

1. Insert the steam rack into the Instant Pot®. Add 1½ cups (350 ml) water.

2. Slice the cabbage into ½-inch-thick (13 mm) slices. In a deep 8-inch (20 cm) round soufflé or casserole dish, make a single layer of the cabbage slices on the bottom. Then layer half of the apple slices. Evenly press in half of the sausage. Repeat with another layer each of cabbage, apple, and sausage. Top with a final layer of cabbage. Cover tightly with aluminum foil.

3. Lock the lid. Press [Manual] and cook on high pressure for 40 minutes. Use the "Quick Release" method to vent the steam, then open the lid.

4. Let rest for 5 minutes. Slice into wedges and serve with a large dollop of mustard and a sprinkle of dill.

Pineapple and Chipotle Pork Tacos

YIELD:
4 servings
PREP TIME:
15 minutes
COOK TIME:
8 hours (slow cook)
1 hour 15 minutes (pressure cook)

INGREDIENTS

PORK

2 teaspoons ground cumin
2 teaspoons chili powder
1 teaspoon dried oregano
1½ teaspoons kosher salt, plus more
    to taste
¼ teaspoon freshly ground black
    pepper
2½ pounds (1.1 kg) pork butt or
    shoulder
¼ cup (60 ml) fresh orange juice
1 canned chipotle chile in adobo
    sauce, finely chopped, plus
    2 tablespoons (30 ml) adobo sauce
3 cloves garlic, finely chopped
1 medium red onion, thinly sliced

SALSA

2 cups (310 g) fresh pineapple cut
    into ½-inch (13 mm) pieces
½ small red onion, finely chopped
½ cup (8 g) chopped fresh cilantro
2 tablespoons (30 ml) fresh lime juice
1 tablespoon (15 ml) extra-virgin
    olive oil
⅛ teaspoon kosher salt

TACOS

8 corn tortillas, warmed

1. In a small bowl, combine the cumin, chili powder, oregano, salt, and pepper.

2. Trim the pork of any extraneous fat. Cut the pork into quarters and season each piece with the spice rub.

3. To the Instant Pot, add the orange juice, chipotle, adobo sauce, garlic, and onion. Stir to combine. Add the pork. Lock the lid.

4. In this step, you have the option to slow-cook or pressure-cook (don't do both!). To slow-cook: press [Slow Cook], leave the vent open, and cook on "More" for 8 hours. To pressure-cook: Press [Manual] and cook on high pressure for 1 hour 15 minutes. Use the "Quick Release" method to vent the steam, then open the lid.

5. Using two forks, shred the pork and stir to combine in the cooking liquid. Season to taste with salt.

6. To make the salsa, in a medium bowl, combine the pineapple, onion, cilantro, lime juice, olive oil, and salt.

7. Fill the tortillas with the shredded pork and top with the salsa.

Sticky and Sweet Sriracha Ribs

Manual   Sauté

YIELD:
4 to 6 servings
PREP TIME:
15 minutes
COOK TIME:
35 minutes

INGREDIENTS

½ cup (120 ml) white vinegar

¼ cup (60 g) packed dark brown sugar,

1 teaspoon chili powder

1 teaspoon paprika (preferably smoked)

1 teaspoon ground cumin

1 teaspoon kosher salt

½ teaspoon freshly ground black pepper

4 pounds (1.8 kg) baby back ribs, cut into individual ribs

3 tablespoons (60 g) apricot jam

1 to 2 tablespoons (15 to 30 ml) sriracha hot sauce

1. Insert the steam rack into the Instant Pot® and add the vinegar.

2. In a small bowl, combine the brown sugar, chili powder, paprika, cumin, salt, and pepper to make the rub.

3. Put the ribs into a large bowl, sprinkle with the rub, and toss to coat evenly. Stack the ribs on the steam rack. Lock the lid. Press [Manual] and cook on high pressure for 20 minutes. Use the "Quick Release" method to vent the steam, then open the lid.

4. Line a rimmed baking sheet with aluminum foil and transfer the ribs to it. Remove the steam rack from the Instant Pot®.

5. Press [Cancel], then press [Sauté]. Whisk the jam and sriracha into the sauce, and simmer until thickened, about 10 minutes. Skim off and discard as much fat as you can from the sauce.

6. Preheat broiler.

7. Spoon half of the sauce over the ribs. Broil until slightly charred, 2 to 3 minutes. Flip the ribs, spoon over the remaining sauce, and broil 2 to 3 minutes more. Serve immediately.

YIELD:

4 servings

PREP TIME:

25 minutes

COOK TIME:

1 hour

Pozole

INGREDIENTS

2 tablespoons (30 ml) extra-virgin
   olive oil

1½ pounds (680 g) boneless pork
   shoulder, trimmed and cut into
   3-inch (7.5 cm) pieces

1½ teaspoons dried oregano

1 teaspoon kosher salt

½ teaspoon freshly ground
   black pepper

4 large cloves garlic, smashed

1 to 2 jalapeños, seeded,
   if desired, and quartered

1 large white onion, chopped

1 pound (454 g) tomatillos, husks
   removed and halved

4 cups (950 ml) less-sodium
   chicken broth

1 bottle (12 ounces, or 355 ml) pale
   lager beer (such as Corona)

1 bunch fresh cilantro (including
   stems), divided

1 can (28 ounces, or 795 g) hominy,
   rinsed and drained

¼ cup (60 ml) fresh lime juice

Sliced radishes, for serving

Diced avocado, for serving

Lime wedges, for serving

1. Turn the Instant Pot® on to [Sauté]. Heat the olive oil. Season
    the pork with the oregano, salt, and pepper, and cook until
    browned, about 6 minutes. Transfer to a plate.

2. Add the garlic, jalapeño, and all but 2 tablespoons of the
    onion, and cook, stirring occasionally, for 3 minutes.

3. Add the tomatillos, chicken broth, beer, and one-third of
    the cilantro. Return the pork to the pot, nestling it in the
    vegetable mixture. Press [Cancel].

4. Lock the lid. Press [Manual] and cook on high pressure for
    45 minutes. Use the "Quick Release" method to vent the
    steam, then open the lid.

5. Remove and discard the cilantro from the pot, and transfer
    the pork to a plate. Add all but ½ cup (8 g) of the remaining
    cilantro and, using a handheld immersion blender (or a
    regular blender), purée the soup.

6. Using 2 forks, break the pork into smaller pieces. Add the
    pork and hominy to the pot. Turn the pot on to [Sauté] and
    cook until the hominy is tender, about 3 minutes. Stir in the
    lime juice.

7. Divide among bowls. Top with radishes, avocado, the
    reserved onion, and the reserved ½ cup (8 g) cilantro (thick
    stems discarded). Serve with lime wedges for squeezing.

Sage and Rosemary Pork Loin

YIELD:
4 servings
PREP TIME:
20 minutes
COOK TIME:
35 minutes

INGREDIENTS

4 cloves garlic, finely chopped

12 fresh sage leaves, chopped

1 tablespoon (2 g) chopped fresh
rosemary

2 tablespoons (30 ml) extra-virgin
olive oil, divided

1½ pounds (680 g) center-cut
pork loin

¾ teaspoon kosher salt

½ teaspoon freshly ground black
pepper

¼ cup (60 ml) dry white wine, such
as Pinot Grigio

1. In a small bowl, combine the garlic, sage, rosemary,
and 1 tablespoon (15 ml) of the olive oil.

2. Spacing about 1 inch (2.5 cm) apart, insert the tip of your
paring knife 6 times and about 1 inch (2.5 cm) deep into the
top of the pork. Fill each opening with some of the herb mixture.
Rub the remaining mixture over the pork and season with the
salt and pepper.

3. Turn the Instant Pot® on to [Sauté]. Heat the remaining
1 tablespoon (15 ml) olive oil. Add the pork and cook until
golden brown on all sides, 10 to 12 minutes. Add the wine.
Press [Cancel].

4. Lock the lid. Press [Manual] and cook on high pressure for
25 minutes. Use the "Quick Release" method to vent the steam,
then open the lid.

5. Transfer the pork to a cutting board and let rest for 5 minutes.
Slice the pork and spoon over some of the jus.

SEAFOOD
MAINS

YIELD:
4 servings
PREP TIME:
20 minutes
COOK TIME:
25 minutes

Jambalaya

INGREDIENTS

1 tablespoon (15 ml) extra-virgin olive oil

2 ribs celery, thinly sliced

1 medium yellow onion, finely chopped

1 green bell pepper, cut into ½-inch (13 mm) pieces

2 cloves garlic, finely chopped

6 ounces (170 g) andouille sausage, cut into ¼-inch-thick (6 mm) pieces

1 can (14½ ounces, or 410 g) diced tomatoes

¾ teaspoon kosher salt

½ teaspoon dried oregano

½ teaspoon dried thyme

¼ teaspoon cayenne pepper

¼ teaspoon freshly ground black pepper

1 bay leaf

1 cup (195 g) long-grain white rice

1 cup (235 ml) water

8 ounces (225 g) medium shrimp, peeled and deveined

¼ cup (15 g) chopped fresh flat-leaf parsley

2 scallions (white and light green parts), thinly sliced

1. Turn the Instant Pot® on to [Sauté]. Heat the olive oil. Add the celery, onion, and bell pepper, and cook, stirring occasionally, until softened, 5 to 6 minutes.

2. Add the garlic and sausage and cook, stirring, for 1 minute. Add the tomatoes, salt, oregano, thyme, cayenne, black pepper, bay leaf, rice, and water, and stir to combine. Press [Cancel].

3. Lock the lid. Press [Manual] and cook on high pressure for 8 minutes. Use the "Quick Release" method to vent the steam, then open the lid. Stir in the shrimp. Lock the lid and let stand for 10 minutes.

4. Discard the bay leaf and stir in the parsley, then sprinkle with the scallions.

YIELD:
4 servings
PREP TIME:
20 minutes
COOK TIME:
15 minutes

Manhattan Clam Chowder

INGREDIENTS

4 slices bacon, chopped

1 yellow onion, chopped

2 cloves garlic, finely chopped

2 ribs celery, cut into ¼-inch
(6 mm) pieces

2 medium carrots, cut into ¼-inch
(6 mm) pieces

1 green bell pepper, cut into
¼-inch (6 mm) pieces

2 cans (6 ounces, or 170 g)
chopped clams

2 bottles (8 ounces, or 235 ml,
each) clam juice

1 can (28 ounces, or 795 g) whole
peeled tomatoes

2 medium Yukon gold potatoes
(about 12 ounces, or 340 g),
cut into ½-inch (13 mm) pieces

6 sprigs fresh thyme

2 bay leaves

¼ teaspoon crushed red pepper
flakes

2 tablespoons (8 g) chopped
fresh flat-leaf parsley

Crusty bread, for serving

1. Turn the Instant Pot® on to [Sauté]. Add the bacon and cook, stirring, for 4 minutes. Add the onion and cook, stirring occasionally until beginning to soften, about 3 minutes. Stir in the garlic and cook for 1 minute. Stir in the celery, carrots, and the bell pepper.

2. Open the cans of clams and drain the juice into a large measuring cup. Set the clams aside. Add enough water to equal 2 cups (475 ml).

3. Add the clam juice–water mixture and the bottles of clam juice to the pot and cook, stirring and scraping up any brown bits, for 1 minute. Add the tomatoes (and their juices) to the pot, crushing them with your hands as you add them. Add the potatoes, thyme, bay leaves, and red pepper flakes. Press [Cancel].

4. Lock the lid. Press [Manual] and cook on high pressure for 4 minutes. Use the "Quick Release" method to vent the steam, then open the pot.

5. Discard the thyme and bay leaves. Stir in the clams and cook until heated through, about 2 minutes. Stir in the parsley and serve immediately with crusty bread.

Red Curry Cod with Green Beans

Manual

YIELD:
4 servings
PREP TIME:
15 minutes
COOK TIME:
5 minutes

INGREDIENTS

1 can (13½ ounces, or 400 ml) unsweetened coconut milk

2 tablespoons (30 g) red Thai curry paste

1 tablespoon (8 g) finely grated fresh ginger

1½ pounds (680 g) cod or halibut fillet, cut into 2-inch (5 cm) pieces

8 ounces (225 g) green beans

½ cup (8 g) fresh cilantro leaves

2 scallions (white and light green parts), thinly sliced

1 lime, quartered

1. To the Instant Pot®, add the coconut milk, curry paste, and ginger, and whisk together. Add the cod. Lay the green beans on top.

2. Lock the lid. Press [Manual] and cook on low pressure for 5 minutes. Use the "Quick Release" method to vent the steam, then open the lid.

3. Top the curry with the cilantro and scallions, and serve with the lime quarters for squeezing.

Italian-Style Seafood Stew

YIELD:
4 to 6 servings
PREP TIME:
20 minutes
COOK TIME:
10 minutes

INGREDIENTS

2 tablespoons (30 ml) extra-virgin olive oil

2 ribs celery, sliced

1 leek (white and light green parts only), sliced into ¼-inch-thick (6 mm) half-moons

1 small bulb fennel, quartered, cored, and sliced

2 large cloves garlic, thinly sliced

2 tablespoons (32 g) tomato paste

1 cup (235 ml) dry white wine, such as Pinot Grigio

1½ pounds (680 g) plum tomatoes, chopped

1 pound (454 g) cod, cut into 2-inch (5 cm) pieces

8 ounces (225 g) large shrimp, peeled and deveined

1 pound (454 g) mussels

1 tablespoon (15 ml) sherry vinegar

Crusty bread, for serving

Chopped fresh flat-leaf parsley, for serving

1. Turn the Instant Pot® on to [Sauté]. Heat the olive oil. Add the celery, leek, and fennel, and cook, stirring occasionally, for 2 minutes. Add the garlic and cook, stirring, for 1 minute. Add the tomato paste and cook, stirring, for 1 minute.

2. Add the wine and tomatoes and toss to combine. Press [Cancel]. Place the cod on top of the vegetables. Press [Manual] and cook on low pressure for 2 minutes. Use the "Quick Release" method to vent the steam, then open the lid.

3. Press [Cancel], then press [Sauté]. Nestle the shrimp in the mixture and cook for 2 minutes. Add the mussels, cover the pot, and cook until the shrimp are opaque throughout and the mussels have opened, about 3 minutes. Press [Cancel], open the lid, and stir in the vinegar.

4. Serve with crusty bread and a sprinkle of parsley.

Salmon with Soy-Ginger Butter and Bok Choy

Sauté   Manual

YIELD:
4 servings
PREP TIME:
10 minutes
COOK TIME:
10 minutes

INGREDIENTS

1 tablespoon (8 g) sesame seeds

¼ cup (½ stick, or 60 g) unsalted butter, at room temperature

1 tablespoon (8 g) grated fresh ginger

2 scallions (white and light green parts), finely chopped

1 teaspoon less-sodium soy sauce

4 fillets (6 ounces, or 170 g, each) salmon

4 baby bok choy, halved lengthwise

1 lemon, quartered

1. Turn the Instant Pot® on to [Sauté]. Add the sesame seeds and toast, stirring often, until golden brown, 2 to 3 minutes. Press [Cancel]. Transfer to a small bowl.

2. Insert the steam rack into the Instant Pot®. Add 1½ cups (350 ml) water.

3. In small bowl, stir together the butter, ginger, scallions, and soy sauce.

4. Tear off a large piece of parchment paper about 20 inches (51 cm) long, and fold it in half. Open it up, place the salmon pieces on one half of the paper, and, dividing evenly, spoon the butter mixture over each piece. Fold the parchment over to cover and make small overlapping folds to seal the edges.

5. Place the parchment packet on the steam rack. Lay the bok choy on top. Lock the lid. Press [Manual] and cook on low pressure for 8 minutes. Use the "Quick Release" method to vent the steam, then open the lid.

6. Divide the bok choy among plates. Lift the packet out and open up. Serve the salmon alongside the bok choy. Top with the sesame seeds and serve with the lemon quarters for squeezing.

Cod Cakes in a Tangy Tomato Sauce

Sauté   Manual

YIELD:
4 servings
PREP TIME:
25 minutes
COOK TIME:
20 minutes

INGREDIENTS

COD CAKES

1 pound (454 g) cod, chopped into
  small pieces
⅓ cup (38 g) dried bread crumbs
2 scallions (white and light green
  parts), finely chopped
2 tablespoons (8 g) chopped fresh
  flat-leaf parsley, plus more for serving
2 tablespoons (2 g) chopped fresh
  cilantro
1 teaspoon finely grated orange zest
½ teaspoon ground cumin
½ teaspoon kosher salt
¼ teaspoon freshly ground
  black pepper
2 large eggs, beaten
2 tablespoons (30 ml) extra-virgin
  olive oil, plus more if necessary

SAUCE

1 can (14½ ounces, or 410 g) crushed
  tomatoes
1 clove garlic, finely chopped
1 teaspoon paprika
1 teaspoon sugar
½ teaspoon kosher salt
¼ teaspoon freshly ground
  black pepper
¼ teaspoon crushed red pepper flakes

1. To make the cod cakes, in a large bowl, combine the cod, bread crumbs, scallions, parsley, cilantro, orange zest, cumin, salt, and pepper. Add the eggs and gently mix in until well combined. Shape into 8 patties about 1 inch (2.5 cm) thick. Refrigerate for 5 minutes.

2. To make the sauce, in a medium bowl, combine the tomatoes, garlic, paprika, sugar, salt, black pepper, and red pepper flakes.

3. Turn the Instant Pot® on to [Sauté]. Heat the olive oil. Add 4 of the cod cakes and cook until golden brown, 2 to 3 minutes per side. Transfer to a plate. Repeat with the remaining cod cakes, adding more olive oil to the pot if necessary.

4. Add the sauce to the pot. Press [Cancel]. In a single layer, nestle the cod cakes in the sauce. Lock the lid. Press [Manual] and cook on low pressure for 8 minutes. Use the "Quick Release" method to vent the steam, then open the lid.

5. Divide the cod cakes and sauce among plates and sprinkle with parsley.

VEGETARIAN MAINS

Layered Vegetable Casserole

Manual

YIELD:
4 servings
PREP TIME:
20 minutes
COOK TIME:
40 minutes

INGREDIENTS

2 tablespoons (30 ml) extra-virgin olive oil, divided, plus more for soufflé dish

1 can (15 ounces, or 425 g) cannellini beans, rinsed and drained

1 clove garlic, peeled

¼ cup (25 g) grated Parmesan cheese, plus more for sprinkling

½ teaspoon kosher salt, divided

1 sweet potato (about 10 ounces, or 280 g), peeled

1 Yukon gold potato (about 8 ounces, or 225 g), unpeeled

1 rutabaga (about 8 ounces, or 225 g), peeled

2 red beets (each about 5 ounces, or 140 g), peeled

1 teaspoon fresh thyme leaves

2 tablespoons (8 g) chopped fresh flat-leaf parsley

⅛ teaspoon freshly ground black pepper

1. Insert the steam rack into the Instant Pot®. Add 1½ cups (350 ml) water. Oil a deep 8-inch (20 cm) round soufflé or casserole dish.

2. In a food processor, purée the beans, garlic, Parmesan, 1 tablespoon (15 ml) of the olive oil, and ¼ teaspoon of the salt until smooth. Spread the purée evenly into the bottom of the dish.

3. Using a chef's knife or mandoline, slice the sweet potato, Yukon gold potato, rutabaga, and beets into about ⅛-inch-thick (3 mm) slices.

4. Arrange the vegetables upright, fitting them snugly together in a pinwheel fashion, alternating as you go. Drizzle with the remaining 1 tablespoon (15 ml) olive oil. Sprinkle with the thyme and the remaining ¼ teaspoon salt.

5. Using aluminum foil, make a "sling" measuring about 3 x 20 inches (7.5 x 51 cm). Use it to lower the dish into the pot. Lock the lid. Press [Manual] and cook on high pressure for 25 minutes. Use the "Natural Release" method for 15 minutes, then vent any remaining steam and open the lid.

6. Sprinkle the casserole with a little more Parmesan and the parsley and pepper.

Vegetable Green Thai Curry

Manual

YIELD:
4 servings
PREP TIME:
15 minutes
COOK TIME:
6 minutes

INGREDIENTS

1 can (13½ ounces, or 400 ml) coconut milk
½ cup (120 ml) water
¾ teaspoon kosher salt
1 medium eggplant (about 1 pound, or 454 g), cut into ¾-inch (2 cm) pieces
1 large sweet potato (about 1 pound, or 454 g), cut into ¾-inch (2 cm) pieces
1 pint grape tomatoes (25 to 30 tomatoes)
1 jalapeño, seeded
1 piece (1 inch, or 2.5 cm) fresh ginger, peeled and sliced
1 clove garlic, peeled
2 cups (32 g) fresh cilantro leaves
3 tablespoons (45 ml) extra-virgin olive oil
Jasmine rice, for serving

1. To the Instant Pot®, add the coconut milk, water, and salt. Add the eggplant, sweet potato, and tomatoes. Lock the lid. Press [Manual] and cook on high pressure for 6 minutes. Use the "Quick Release" method to release the steam, then open the lid.

2. In a food processor, purée the jalapeño, ginger, garlic, cilantro, and oil until smooth. Stir into the vegetables.

3. Serve the curry over jasmine rice.

Artichokes Stuffed with Parmesan Bread Crumbs

Manual

YIELD:
4 servings
PREP TIME:
20 minutes
COOK TIME:
20 minutes

INGREDIENTS

4 medium globe artichokes

1 cup (100 g) grated Parmesan cheese

¾ cup (90 g) dried bread crumbs

½ cup (30 g) chopped fresh flat-leaf parsley

¼ cup (24 g) chopped fresh mint

2 cloves garlic, finely chopped

¾ teaspoon kosher salt

¼ teaspoon freshly ground black pepper

½ cup (120 ml) extra-virgin olive oil, plus more for drizzling

1 pint grape tomatoes (25 to 30 tomatoes), cut into small pieces

1. Insert the steam rack into the Instant Pot®. Add 1½ cups (350 ml) water.

2. Trim the top quarter from the artichokes and discard. Trim and reserve the stems so the artichokes sit flat. Place the artichokes and stems in the steam rack and lock the lid. Press [Manual] and cook on high pressure for 20 minutes. Use the "Quick Release" method to vent the steam, then open the lid. Let cool to room temperature.

3. Gently spread apart the leaves of the artichokes. Use a melon baller to scoop out and discard the chokes. Chop the stems.

4. In a medium bowl, combine the chopped stems, Parmesan, bread crumbs, parsley, mint, garlic, salt, and pepper. Stir in the olive oil, then fold in the tomatoes.

5. Fill the center of each artichoke with bread crumb mixture, then spoon the remaining mixture in between the leaves. Drizzle a little more oil over the top, and serve.

Minestrone Soup

YIELD:
6 servings
PREP TIME:
15 minutes
COOK TIME:
15 minutes

INGREDIENTS

1 tablespoon (15 ml) extra-virgin
   olive oil
1 medium yellow onion,
   finely chopped
2 cloves garlic, finely chopped
2 tablespoons (32 g) tomato paste
2 containers (32 ounces, or
   950 ml, each) less-sodium
   vegetable broth
2 medium carrots, sliced into
   half-moons
2 ribs celery, sliced
2 medium red potatoes (about
   8 ounces, or 225 g), cut into
   1-inch (2.5 cm) pieces
¼ small head Savoy cabbage,
   cored and cut into 1-inch
   (2.5 cm) pieces
1 cup (93 g) ditalini or other
   small pasta
½ teaspoon kosher salt
½ teaspoon freshly ground
   black pepper
1 can (15 ounces, or 425 g)
   kidney beans, rinsed and drained
1 cup (130 g) frozen peas, thawed
1 bunch spinach, thick stems
   discarded
Grated Parmesan cheese,
   for serving
Prepared pesto, for serving

1. Turn the Instant Pot® on to [Sauté]. Heat the olive oil. Add the onion and cook, stirring occasionally, for 3 minutes. Add the garlic and cook, stirring, for 1 minute. Add the tomato paste and cook, stirring, for 1 minute.

2. Add the vegetable broth and cook, stirring and scraping up any brown bits, for 1 minute. Add the carrots, celery, potatoes, cabbage, pasta, salt, and pepper. Press [Cancel].

3. Lock the lid. Press [Manual] and cook on high pressure for 3 minutes. Use the "Quick Release" method to vent the steam, then open the lid.

4. Add the beans and peas, and cook until heated through, about 2 minutes. Add the spinach and cook until beginning to wilt, about 1 minute.

5. Ladle into bowls and serve with Parmesan and a dollop of pesto.

Spinach and Herb Lasagna

YIELD:
4 to 6 servings
PREP TIME:
20 minutes
COOK TIME
25 minutes

INGREDIENTS

1 large egg

½ teaspoon kosher salt

½ teaspoon freshly ground black pepper

1 pound (454 g) ricotta cheese

¼ cup (25 g) grated Pecorino cheese

8 ounces (225 g) fresh mozzarella cheese, coarsely shredded

2 cups (60 g) baby spinach, chopped

¼ cup (15 g) chopped fresh flat-leaf parsley

¼ cup (10 g) chopped fresh basil

2½ cups (595 ml) your favorite marinara sauce

8 no-boil lasagna noodles

1. Insert the steam rack into the Instant Pot® and add 1½ cups (350 ml) water. In a medium bowl, beat the egg with the salt and pepper. Add the ricotta, Pecorino, and ½ cup (60 g) of the mozzarella, and mix to combine. Fold in the spinach, parsley, and basil.

2. Spread ½ cup (120 ml) of the marinara on the bottom of a deep 8-inch (20 cm) round soufflé or casserole dish. Top with 2 noodles, breaking them to fit as necessary, then spread ½ cup (120 ml) of the marinara over the top. Dollop with one-third of the ricotta mixture and sprinkle with one-quarter of the remaining mozzarella.

3. Top with 2 noodles, breaking them to fit as necessary, and spread ½ cup (120 ml) of the marinara and another one-third each of the ricotta mixture and the mozzarella. Repeat once more. Finish by topping with the remaining 2 noodles, ½ cup (120 g) of sauce, and a quarter of mozzarella.

4. Cover the dish with aluminum foil. Using another piece of foil, make a "sling" measuring about 3 x 20 inches (7.5 x 51 cm). Use it to lower the pan into the pot.

5. Lock the lid. Press [Manual] and cook on high pressure for 10 minutes. Use the "Natural Release" method for 15 minutes, then vent any remaining steam and open the lid. Lift the lasagna from the pot and discard the foil.

6. If desired, preheat broiler and broil the lasagna until the cheese is golden brown, 2 to 3 minutes.

Broccoli and Parmesan Farrotto

Sauté   Manual

YIELD:
4 servings
PREP TIME:
20 minutes
COOK TIME:
25 minutes

INGREDIENTS

2 tablespoons (30 ml)
extra-virgin olive oil

1 medium yellow onion,
finely chopped

½ teaspoon kosher salt, divided

½ teaspoon freshly ground black
pepper, divided, plus more for
serving

2 cloves garlic, finely chopped

1 cup (208 g) farro

½ cup (120 ml) dry white wine,
such as Pinot Grigio

3 cups (700 ml) less-sodium
vegetable broth or water

1 small bunch broccoli, cut into
small florets

½ cup (50 g) grated Parmesan
cheese, plus more for serving

1. Turn the Instant Pot® on to [Sauté]. Heat the olive oil. Add the onion, ¼ teaspoon of the salt, and ¼ teaspoon of the pepper, and cook, stirring occasionally, for 3 minutes. Add the garlic and cook, stirring, for 1 minute. Add the farro and stir to coat in the oil.

2. Add the wine and simmer until it has nearly evaporated, 2 to 3 minutes. Add the broth and press [Cancel]. Lock the lid. Press [Manual] and cook on high pressure for 10 minutes. Use the "Quick Release" method to vent the steam, then open the lid.

3. Press [Cancel], then press [Sauté]. Once the mixture is simmering, add the broccoli and mix to combine. Cover and cook for 3 minutes. Uncover and simmer until the broccoli is tender, about 2 minutes more. Press [Cancel].

4. In 2 additions, fold in the Parmesan, then season with the remaining ¼ teaspoon salt and ¼ teaspoon pepper. Serve sprinkled with a little more Parmesan.

Baked Sweet Potatoes with Green Apple Slaw

YIELD:
4 servings
PREP TIME:
15 minutes
COOK TIME:
35 minutes

INGREDIENTS

4 sweet potatoes (about
   12 ounces, or 340 g, each)
1 medium fennel bulb,
   thinly sliced
1 green apple, such as Granny
   Smith, cut into 1-inch (2.5 cm)
   sticks
3 tablespoons (45 ml) fresh
   lemon juice
3 tablespoons (45 ml) extra-virgin
   olive oil
¼ cup (15 g) chopped fresh
   flat-leaf parsley
2 scallions (white and light green
   parts), thinly sliced
¼ cup (37 g) roasted almonds
¼ teaspoon kosher salt
⅛ teaspoon freshly ground
   black pepper

1. Insert the steam rack into the Instant Pot®. Add 1½ cups
   (350 ml) water.

2. Pierce the potatoes several times with a fork, then place on the
   steam rack. Lock the lid. Press [Manual] and cook on high pressure
   for 20 minutes. Use the "Natural Release" method for 15 minutes,
   then vent any remaining steam and open the lid.

3. In a medium bowl, combine the fennel, apple, lemon juice, olive
   oil, parsley, scallions, almonds, salt, and pepper for the slaw.

4. Make a slit in the top of each potato and gently squeeze to open
   each one up. Spoon the slaw over the potatoes.

Yogurt Dip 3 Ways

INGREDIENTS

SPINACH AND PARMESAN DIP

1 clove garlic, finely chopped

½ teaspoon kosher salt

1 cup (230 g) plain yogurt (see page 26 for instructions on how to make yogurt)

¼ cup (25 g) grated Parmesan cheese

½ teaspoon finely grated lemon zest

¼ teaspoon freshly ground black pepper

1 package (10 ounces, or 280 g) frozen leaf spinach, thawed

Potato chips, for serving

Cut vegetables, for serving

ROASTED RED PEPPER
AND FETA DIP

1 small clove garlic, peeled

1 jar (6 ounces, or 170 g) roasted red peppers, drained and patted dry

8 ounces (225 g) feta cheese, crumbled

½ cup (115 g) plain yogurt (see page 26 for instructions on how to make yogurt)

½ teaspoon finely grated lemon zest

¼ teaspoon crushed red pepper flakes

Pretzels, for serving

Cut vegetables, for serving

Spinach and Parmesan Dip

YIELD: 6 servings PREP TIME: 10 minute

1. Sprinkle the garlic with the salt and, using the side of a knife, rub the salt into the garlic to create a paste. Transfer to a medium bowl and add the yogurt, Parmesan, lemon zest, and pepper, and whisk to combine.

2. Squeeze any excess liquid from the spinach, then coarsely chop. Add to the bowl and mix to combine. Serve with potato chips and vegetables.

Roasted Red Pepper and Feta Dip

YIELD: 6 servings PREP TIME: 10 minutes

In a food processor, pulse the garlic and red peppers until finely chopped. Add the feta, yogurt, lemon zest, and red pepper flakes, and purée until smooth. Serve with pretzels and vegetables.

>> CONTINUED ON PAGE 150

TZATZIKI

¼ seedless cucumber, cut into
  ¼-inch (6 mm) pieces
2 scallions (white and light green
  parts), finely chopped
½ teaspoon finely grated
  lemon zest
1 tablespoon (15 ml) fresh
  lemon juice
¼ teaspoon kosher salt
¼ teaspoon freshly ground
  black pepper
1 cup (230 g) plain yogurt (see
  page 26 for instructions on
  how to make yogurt)
2 tablespoons (8 g) chopped
  fresh dill
2 tablespoons (12 g) chopped
  fresh mint
Pita chips, for serving
Cut vegetables, for serving

Tzatziki

YIELD: 4 to 6 servings PREP TIME: 15 minutes

In a small bowl, toss together the cucumber, scallions, lemon zest,
lemon juice, salt, and pepper. Stir in the yogurt, dill, and mint.
Serve with pita chips and vegetables.

Cheesy Pasta and Kale

YIELD:
4 servings
PREP TIME:
10 minutes
COOK TIME:
15 minutes

INGREDIENTS

12 ounces (340 g) mezze rigatoni

½ cup (120 g) mascarpone cheese, at room temperature

1 tablespoon (11 g) Dijon mustard

⅛ teaspoon freshly grated nutmeg

1½ cups (180 g) grated Gruyère cheese

¼ cup (25 g) grated Parmesan cheese

3 cups (200 g) baby kale

½ teaspoon freshly ground black pepper

¼ teaspoon kosher salt

1. Put the pasta and 4 cups (950 ml) water in the Instant Pot®. Lock the lid. Press [Manual] and cook on high pressure for 5 minutes. Use the "Natural Release" method for 5 minutes, then vent any remaining steam and open the lid. Press [Cancel].

2. Reserve ½ cup (120 ml) of the pasta water, then drain the pasta and return it to the pot. Press [Sauté]. Add the mascarpone, mustard, and nutmeg, and toss until the pasta is evenly coated.

3. Add the Gruyère and Parmesan, and toss until the cheeses melt. Stir in some of the reserved pasta water if the sauce is too thick.

4. Add the kale and cook, tossing until just wilted, for about 2 minutes. Season with the pepper and salt. Press [Cancel] and serve immediately.

DESSERTS

Double Chocolate Cheesecake

YIELD:
6 servings

PREP TIME:
20 minutes

COOK TIME:
1 hour (plus 6 hours refrigeration time)

INGREDIENTS

CRUST
Nonstick vegetable oil cooking spray
22 chocolate wafer cookies
1 tablespoon (13 g) granulated sugar
¼ teaspoon ground cinnamon
¼ cup (½ stick, or 60g), unsalted butter, melted

FILLING
1¼ cups (220 g) semisweet chocolate chips
2 packages (8 ounces, or 225 g each) cream cheese, at room temperature
¾ cup (150 g) granulated sugar
3 large eggs
¼ cup (60 g) sour cream
1 teaspoon pure vanilla extract

WHIPPED CREAM
¾ cup (175 ml) heavy cream
3 tablespoons (23 g) confectioners' sugar

TOPPING
A small hunk of chocolate, for shaving

1. Insert the steam rack into the Instant Pot®. Add 1½ cups (350 ml) water.

2. To make the crust, coat a 7-inch (18 cm) springform pan with cooking spray. Use a food processor or a resealable plastic bag and a rolling pin to grind the cookies. Mix in the sugar, cinnamon, and butter.

3. Using a flat-bottomed glass, press the crumbs evenly on the bottom and 1 inch (2.5 cm) up the sides of the pan. Freeze the crust while you make the filling.

4. To make the filling, in a medium microwave-safe bowl melt the chocolate chips on high, stirring every 30 seconds, until melted and smooth, about 60 seconds total. Let cool to room temperature, keeping the chocolate warm enough to be pourable.

5. In a large bowl, use an electric mixer on medium speed to beat the cream cheese until smooth and creamy. Beat in the sugar until smooth. Add the eggs, one at a time, beating well after each addition and scraping down the sides of the bowl as needed. Beat in the sour cream and vanilla.

6. With the mixer on low speed, pour in the chocolate and mix in completely. Pour the filling into the prepared crust.

CONTINUED ON PAGE 156 >

7. Tightly wrap the entire pan in aluminum foil. Using another piece of foil, make a "sling" measuring about 3 x 20 inches (7.5 x 51 cm). Use it to lower the pan into the pot.

8. Lock the lid. Press [Manual] and cook on high pressure for 57 minutes. Use the "Quick Release" method to vent the steam, then open the lid.

9. Lift the pan out and remove the foil (the cheesecake will be slightly wobbly in the center). Let cool on a wire cooling rack for 25 minutes, then run a knife around the edges to loosen it from the pan. Refrigerate for at least 6 hours or overnight, until completely set.

10. To make the whipped cream, in a medium bowl, whisk together the cream and confectioners' sugar until soft peaks form.

11. To serve the cheesecake, remove the ring. Spread the whipped cream over the top of the cheesecake, leaving a 1-inch (2.5 cm) border. Use a vegetable peeler to shave the hunk of chocolate over the top.

Chocolate-Peanut Butter Brownies

Manual

YIELD:
10 servings
PREP TIME:
15 minutes
COOK TIME:
55 minutes

INGREDIENTS

Nonstick vegetable oil
  cooking spray
4 ounces (115 g) bittersweet
  chocolate, chopped
¾ cup (1½ sticks, or 180 g)
  unsalted butter
2 teaspoons instant
  espresso powder
1 teaspoon pure vanilla
  extract
3 large eggs
1 cup (200 g) sugar
1 cup (120 g) all-purpose flour
½ teaspoon kosher salt
¼ teaspoon baking powder
1 cup (175 g) peanut butter chips
½ cup (88 g) bittersweet
  chocolate chips

1. Insert the steam rack into the Instant Pot®. Add 1½ cups (350 ml) water. Coat a deep 8-inch (20 cm) round soufflé or casserole dish with cooking spray.

2. In a medium microwave-safe bowl, melt the chocolate and butter on high, stirring every 30 seconds, until melted and smooth, about 60 seconds total. Stir in the espresso powder and vanilla.

3. In a large bowl, beat the eggs and sugar until combined. Add the chocolate mixture and mix to combine. Add the flour, salt, and baking powder, and mix until fully incorporated. Fold in the peanut butter chips and chocolate chips, then scrape the batter into the prepared dish.

4. Cover the dish with aluminum foil. Using another piece of foil, make a "sling" measuring about 3 x 20 inches (7.5 x 51 cm). Use it to lower the dish into the pot.

5. Lock the lid. Press [Manual] and cook on high pressure for 45 minutes. Use the "Natural Release" method for 10 minutes, then vent any remaining steam and open the lid. Transfer the dish to a wire cooling rack, uncover, and let cool for at least 20 minutes before serving.

Lemon Soufflé Pudding Cake

Manual

YIELD:
6 servings
PREP TIME:
10 minutes
COOK TIME:
45 minutes

INGREDIENTS

2 tablespoons (30 g) unsalted butter, melted, plus more for soufflé dish

2 large eggs

¾ cup (150 g) granulated sugar, divided

Grated zest of 2 lemons

⅓ cup (80 ml) fresh lemon juice

¼ cup (30 g) all-purpose flour

⅛ teaspoon kosher salt

1¼ cups (300 ml) whole milk

1 cup (235 ml) heavy cream

¼ cup (30 g) confectioners' sugar, plus more for dusting

1. Insert the steam rack into the Instant Pot®. Add 1½ cups (350 ml) water. Butter a deep 8-inch (20 cm) round soufflé or casserole dish.

2. Separate the egg whites and yolks into 2 large bowls.

3. To the egg yolks, whisk in ½ cup (100 g) of the sugar. Add the lemon zest, lemon juice, flour, and salt, and whisk together. Whisk in the milk, then the melted butter.

4. Using an electric mixer, beat the egg whites on medium-high speed until opaque and foamy. With the mixer running, slowly pour in the remaining ¼ cup (50 g) sugar. Beat until shiny, stiff peaks form. Fold one-third of the whites into the lemon mixture. Then gently fold in the remaining whites. Pour the batter into the prepared dish.

5. Cover the dish with aluminum foil, tenting it to allow room for the soufflé to rise. Using another piece of foil, make a "sling" measuring about 3 x 20 inches (7.5 x 51 cm). Use it to lower the dish into the pot.

6. Lock the lid. Press [Manual] and cook on high pressure for 45 minutes. Use the "Quick Release" method to vent the steam, then open the lid. Lift the dish out and uncover.

7. In a medium bowl, whisk together the cream and confectioners' sugar until soft peaks form.

8. Dust the soufflé with confectioners' sugar and serve warm with the whipped cream.

Sticky Toffee Pudding

Manual

YIELD:
6 servings
PREP TIME:
20 minutes
COOK TIME:
35 minutes

INGREDIENTS

PUDDING

6 tablespoons (90 g) unsalted butter, melted, plus more for soufflé dish
8 dried (but pliable) Medjool dates, pitted
¾ cup (180 ml) very hot water
1 teaspoon baking soda
2 tablespoons (30 ml) dark rum
½ cup (100 g) granulated sugar
2 large eggs
1 cup (120 g) all-purpose flour
¼ teaspoon kosher salt

TOFFEE SAUCE

¼ cup (½ stick, or 60 g) unsalted butter
½ cup (115 g) packed dark brown sugar
¼ cup (60 ml) heavy cream
½ teaspoon pure vanilla extract
Pinch kosher salt

1. Insert the steam rack into the Instant Pot®. Add 1½ cups (350 ml) water. Butter a deep 8-inch (20 cm) round soufflé or casserole dish.

2. To make the pudding, in a medium bowl, combine the dates, hot water, baking soda, and rum. Let stand until the dates are very soft, about 15 minutes.

3. In a large bowl, whisk together the sugar and melted butter. Whisk in the eggs, one at a time. Stir in the flour and salt.

4. In a food processor or blender, purée the dates and liquid until smooth. Pour into the batter and stir until incorporated. Pour the batter into the prepared dish.

5. Cover the dish tightly with aluminum foil. Using another piece of foil, make a "sling" measuring about 3 x 20 inches (7.5 x 51 cm). Use it to lower the dish into the pot.

6. Lock the lid. Press [Manual] and cook on high pressure for 30 minutes. Use the "Quick Release" method to vent the steam, then open the lid. Lift the dish out and uncover.

7. To make the toffee sauce, rinse out and dry the inner pot. Press [Sauté]. Add the butter and melt. Add the brown sugar and whisk until melted, about 30 seconds. Whisk in the cream until incorporated and then let simmer, whisking often, for 1 minute. Press [Cancel]. Whisk in the vanilla and salt.

8. Pour the toffee sauce over the pudding and spoon into individual bowls.

Warm Chocolate Fudge Cakes

Manual

YIELD:
6 servings
PREP TIME:
15 minutes
COOK TIME:
20 minutes

INGREDIENTS

Nonstick vegetable oil cooking
  spray
½ cup (1 stick, or 120 g) unsalted
  butter
½ cup (100 g) sugar
¼ cup (60 ml) heavy cream
4 ounces (115 g) semisweet
  chocolate chips
1 teaspoon pure vanilla extract
2 large eggs
2 tablespoons (12 g) unsweetened
  cocoa powder
1 tablespoon (8 g) all-purpose flour
Pinch kosher salt
Vanilla ice cream, for serving

1. Insert the steam rack into the Instant Pot®. Add 1½ cups (350 ml) water. Coat six 4-ounce (120 ml) heatproof ramekins with cooking spray.

2. In a small saucepan, combine the butter, sugar, and cream over medium heat. Heat the mixture, stirring often, until melted. Add the chocolate chips and vanilla and remove from the heat. Let stand for 1 minute, then whisk until creamy and smooth.

3. In a medium bowl, whisk together the eggs, cocoa powder, flour, and salt. Whisk in the chocolate mixture until incorporated.

4. Dividing evenly, pour the batter into the prepared ramekins. Cover each tightly with aluminum foil. Place in the pot, stacking them as necessary.

5. Lock the lid. Press [Manual] and cook on high pressure for 15 minutes. Use the "Quick Release" method to vent the steam, then open the lid. Lift the ramekins out and uncover.

6. Unmold the cakes and serve warm, topped with ice cream.

Dulce de Leche Shortbread Cookies

YIELD:
30 sandwich cookies
PREP TIME:
5 minutes
COOK TIME:
45 minutes

INGREDIENTS

1 can (14 ounces, or 425 ml)
    sweetened condensed milk
60 small shortbread cookies

1. Insert the steam rack into the Instant Pot®. Pour the condensed milk into a 16-ounce (475 ml) canning jar with a tight-fitting lid. Close the jar. Place the jar on the rack and add enough water to come halfway up the sides of the jar (about 12 cups, or 2.9 L).

2. Lock the lid. Press [Manual] and cook on high pressure for 35 minutes. Use the "Natural Release" method for 10 minutes, then vent any remaining steam and open the lid. Remove the jar from the pot and stir. (This will yield about 1¼ cups, or 350 ml.)

3. Let the dulce de leche cool for 5 minutes, then sandwich between the cookies.

Pumpkin Spice Cake

Manual

YIELD:
8 servings
PREP TIME:
20 minutes
COOK TIME:
50 minutes

INGREDIENTS

CAKE

Nonstick vegetable oil cooking
  spray
1½ cups (180 g) all-purpose flour
1 teaspoon baking powder
½ teaspoon baking soda
½ teaspoon kosher salt
½ teaspoon ground ginger
¼ teaspoon ground cinnamon
1/8 teaspoon ground cloves
1/8 teaspoon ground nutmeg
½ cup (1 stick, or 120 g) unsalted
  butter, at room temperature
½ cup (100 g) granulated sugar
2 large eggs
1 teaspoon pure vanilla extract
¾ cup (184 g) canned pure
  pumpkin
¼ cup (85 g) unsulfured molasses

GLAZE

1 cup (100 g) confectioners' sugar
4 teaspoons whole milk, plus more
  if necessary
½ teaspoon pure vanilla extract
1 lemon

1. Insert the steam rack into the Instant Pot®. Add 1½ cups (350 ml) water. Coat a 7-inch (18 cm) angel food cake pan with cooking spray.

2. In a medium bowl, whisk together the flour, baking powder, baking soda, salt, ginger, cinnamon, cloves, and nutmeg.

3. Using an electric mixer on medium-high speed, in a large bowl, beat the butter and sugar until light and fluffy, about 3 minutes. Beat in the eggs, one at a time, then the vanilla. Beat in the pumpkin and the molasses. Reduce the mixer speed to low and gradually add the flour mixture, mixing just until incorporated. Scrape the mixture into the prepared pan.

4. Cover the pan with aluminum foil. Using another piece of foil, make a "sling" measuring about 3 x 20 inches (7.5 x 51 cm). Use it to lower the pan into the pot.

5. Lock the lid. Press [Manual] and cook on high pressure for 50 minutes. Use the "Quick Release" method to vent the steam, then open the lid. Transfer the pan to a wire cooling rack, remove the foil, and let cool for 20 minutes before unmolding. Let cool completely.

6. Just before serving, make the glaze. In a small bowl, whisk together the confectioners' sugar, milk, and vanilla extract until smooth and pourable (adding more milk, a few drops at a time, if necessary). Spoon the glaze over the top of the cake and let drizzle down the sides. Using a vegetable peeler, peel the lemon zest in strips. Thinly slice the strips crosswise and sprinkle over the cake.

Crème Brûlée

YIELD:
6 servings
PREP TIME:
15 minutes
COOK TIME:
20 minutes (plus 4 hours refrigeration time)

INGREDIENTS

5 large egg yolks
⅔ cup (130 g) plus 6 tablespoons (75 g) sugar, divided
½ vanilla bean, split lengthwise, or ½ teaspoon pure vanilla extract
2¼ cups (535 ml) heavy cream
¼ cup (60 ml) whole milk

1. Insert the steam rack into the Instant Pot®. Add 1½ cups (350 ml) water.

2. In a large bowl, whisk together the egg yolks and ⅔ cup (130 g) of the sugar. Scrape the seeds out of the vanilla bean and whisk into the egg mixture. Whisk in the cream and milk.

3. Pour the custard into six 4-ounce (120 ml) shallow ramekins. Cover each tightly with aluminum foil. Place on the rack, stacking them as necessary.

4. Lock the lid. Press [Manual] and cook on low pressure for 18 minutes. Use the "Quick Release" method to vent the steam, then open the lid. Lift the ramekins out (they will be slightly wobbly in the middle). Let cool on a wire cooling rack for 25 minutes. Refrigerate, covered, for at least 4 hours or overnight, until completely cool and set.

5. To serve, sprinkle the top of each custard with 1 tablespoon (13 g) of the sugar. Use a kitchen blowtorch or the oven broiler to caramelize the sugar until dark golden brown. Serve immediately.

INDEX

ABOUT THE AUTHORS

SARA QUESSENBERRY is a cook, food stylist, recipe developer, and author. Sara co-wrote *The Good Neighbor Cookbook*, which was voted Best Books 2011: Cooking by *Library Journal*. She also collaborated on the *New York Times* best-seller *The Can't Cook Book*. She is currently the food/web director of JessicaSeinfeld.com, a website for beginner cooks. Her next collaboration with Seinfeld is *Food Swings: 125+ Recipes to Enjoy Your Life of Virtue & Vice*.

KATE MERKER is a cook, editor, recipe developer, culinary producer, and author. Throughout her career, Kate has worked in the kitchens of internationally renowned restaurants as well as in test kitchens for cookbooks, magazines, and TV studios. She is currently the Food & Nutrition Director of *Woman's Day* magazine, where her ultimate goal is to help readers get dinner on the table efficiently, healthfully, and happily. The author of three Woman's Day cookbooks (*Easy Everyday Dinners*, *Easy Everyday Lighter Dinners*, and *Recipe Remix*) and the editor of *Best Recipes: Easy, Delicious Meals from Real Simple*, Kate is currently working on her fourth cookbook for *Woman's Day*.

ABOUT
INSTANT POT®

The Instant Pot® Company was founded in 2009 by a team of Canadian technology veterans who set out to explore the food preparation category based on their own personal experiences. Their objective was to find solutions that would enable busy families and professionals to prepare quality food in less time, promoting better eating and reducing the consumption of fast food.

In late 2010, after eighteen grueling months of research, design, and development, they introduced the Instant Pot® CSG60, the company's first multi-programmable electric cooker. The introduction was a great success, propelling the team to continue to develop even more versatile products to meet the growing needs of consumers with active, busy, healthy, and environmentally conscious lifestyles. Each subsequent Instant Pot® product introduction has raised the bar on functionality, user-friendliness, and safety.

The Instant Pot® products are truly tools for a new lifestyle and especially cater to the needs of health-minded individuals, those with special dietary restrictions, the do-it-yourself food enthusiasts, and anyone looking to save time in the kitchen while providing nutritious, well-balanced meals.